WISDOM KEYS FOR EVERY DAY

INSPIRED FROM SCRIPTURES.

365 DAYS

Volume 1

Lemun Yatu

Copyright © 2016 Lemun Yatu

All rights reserved.

ISBN:10:1537110772

ISBN-13:9781537110776

DEDICATION

This book is dedicated to the almighty God the foundation and master of all wisdom.

Foreword

People acquire wisdom in different ways. Some gain wisdom through experience, others through directly listening to elderly people or those that are considered repository of wisdom. Yet through the ages, we have seen that the Bible has remained an inexhaustible ocean of wisdom that many Christians and non-Christians have referred to. Lemun has leaned on the Bible as the foundation of his daily dose of wisdom offered to us, backing every day's word of wisdom with the scriptural reference that has influenced the word. This confirms that the words of wisdom you will read in the pages of this book, have been tried and proven for thousands of years, so they are trustworthy and guaranteed to lead the reader aright.

In these days that the Bible is scorned by many as a book that is 'no longer relevant for this age of technological enlightenment', Lemun has proven that it is living and still speaking to us. The nuggets of wisdom he offers are such that for each day, there is something for the reader to study and meditate on. These are words from the heart of a man who has found strength, encouragement, and stability in the word of God.

Rev. Kefas Amos Tang'an
COCIN London

ACKNOWLEDGMENTS

I wish to acknowledge the effort of all those who contributed to the success of this book. I may not be able to mention all of you by names but all the same, I am exceedingly grateful for your great contributions.

God bless you all.

Lemun Yatu

DAY 1

"There are far too many battles to fight in life; choose yours carefully and wisely"

[15] He said: "Listen, King Jehoshaphat and all who live in Judah and Jerusalem! This is what the LORD says to you: 'Do not be afraid or discouraged because of this vast army. For the battle is not yours, but God's.

2 Chronicles 20:15

DAY 2

"The person who has a lot to do with you-is you. Never give up on yourself".

[12] I know how to be abased, and I know how to abound. Everywhere and in all things I have learned both to be full and to be hungry, both to abound and to suffer need. [13] I can do all things through Christ[a] who strengthens me.

Philippians 4:12-14

DAY 3

"The devil is an opportunist; he waits for opportunities to take opportunity. Don't give him one".

[13] When the devil had finished all this tempting, he left him until an opportune time.

Luke 4:13

DAY 4

"People don't only want to hear the good news from you, but also want to see the good news in you- just live it".

³ He got into one of the boats, the one belonging to Simon, and asked him to put out a little from shore. Then he sat down and taught the people from the boat. ⁸ When Simon Peter saw this, he fell at Jesus' knees and said, "Go away from me, Lord; I am a sinful man!"

Luke 5:3, 8

DAY 5

"It is not only what you say, but what you live, that pulls many to you. Just live your words".

[11] *So they pulled their boats up on shore, left everything and followed him.*

Luke 5:11

DAY 6

"The presence of God in your life, makes all the difference in life. Insist on having it".

[15] Then Moses said to him, "If your Presence does not go with us, do not send us up from here.

Exodus 33: 15

DAY 7

"When he is not at the centre of your focus, you easily lose focus. Get him back at the centre."

[15] Then he said to them, "Watch out! Be on your guard against all kinds of greed; life does not consist in an abundance of possessions." [16] And he told them this parable: "The ground of a certain rich man yielded an abundant harvest. [17] He thought to himself, 'What shall I do? I have no place to store my crops.'

[18] "Then he said, 'This is what I'll do. I will tear down my barns and build bigger ones, and there I will store my surplus grain. [19] And I'll say to myself, "You have plenty of grain laid up for many years. Take life easy; eat, drink and be merry."'

[20] "But God said to him, 'You fool! This very night your life will be demanded from you. Then who will get what you

have prepared for yourself?' [21] *"This is how it will be with whoever stores up things for themselves but is not rich toward God."*

Luke 12:15-21

DAY 8

"If you cannot figure out the minor, why worry about the major? Just leave it to God, let him sort it out"

^{24} Consider the ravens: They do not sow or reap, they have no storeroom or barn; yet God feeds them. And how much more valuable you are than birds! ^{25} Who of you by worrying can add a single hour to your life[a]? ^{26} Since you cannot do this very little thing, why do you worry about the rest?

^{27} "Consider how the wild flowers grow. They do not labor or spin. Yet I tell you, not even Solomon in all his splendor was dressed like one of these. ^{28} If that is how God clothes the grass of the field, which is here today, and tomorrow is thrown into the fire, how much more will he clothe you—you of little faith

Luke 12:24-28

DAY 9

"When the pursuit of God overwhelms your life, then answers to your needs overtake your life. Seek him first always".

[29] And do not set your heart on what you will eat or drink; do not worry about it. [30] For the pagan world runs after all such things, and your Father knows that you need them. [31] But seek his kingdom, and these things will be given to you as well.

Luke 12:29-31

DAY 10

"Don't spend your life and time on just what you were trained to do, but discover what you were born to do, and squander the rest of your life on it".

[19] Though I am free and belong to no one, I have made myself a slave to everyone, to win as many as possible. [20] To the Jews I became like a Jew, to win the Jews. To those under the law I became like one under the law (though I myself am not under the law), so as to win those under the law. [21] To those not having the law I became like one not having the law (though I am not free from God's law but am under Christ's law), so as to win those not having the law. [22] To the weak I became weak, to win the weak. I have become all things to all people so that by all possible means I might save some. [23] I do all this for the sake of the gospel that I may share in its blessings.

1 Corinthians 9:19-23

DAY 11

"If you let it away the first time, losing it the second time will be normal. Keep it well, whatever it is".

²⁵ Meanwhile, Simon Peter was still standing there warming himself. So they asked him, "You aren't one of his disciples too, are you?" He denied it, saying, "I am not." ²⁶ One of the high priest's servants, a relative of the man whose ear Peter had cut off, challenged him, "Didn't I see you with him in the garden?" ²⁷ Again Peter denied it, and at that moment a rooster began to crow.

John 18:25-27

DAY 12

"Your place in life is the function of your purpose for life. Live purposefully"

[34] *"Salt is good, but if it loses its saltiness, how can it be made salty again? [35] It is fit neither for the soil nor for the manure pile; it is thrown out. "Whoever has ears to hear, let them hear"*

Luke 14:34-35

DAY 13

"You cannot help but be jealous of what others have or are being given, if you don't know what you have."

²⁸ "The older brother became angry and refused to go in. So his father went out and pleaded with him. ²⁹ But he answered his father, 'Look! All these years I've been slaving for you and never disobeyed your orders. Yet you never gave me even a young goat so I could celebrate with my friends. ³⁰ But when this son of yours who has squandered your property with prostitutes comes home, you kill the fattened calf for him!' ³¹ "'My son,' the father said, 'you are always with me, and everything I have is yours. ³² But we had to celebrate and be glad, because this brother of yours was dead and is alive again; he was lost and is found.'"

Luke 15:11-12, 28-32

DAY 14

"Until you believe him enough, to know that His presence would make a difference in your situation, you limit what he could do in your life. Just stretch your faith beyond the limits".

³² When Mary reached the place where Jesus was and saw him, she fell at his feet and said, "Lord, if you had been here, my brother would not have died

John 11:32

DAY 15

"Despite his Lordship over our situation and circumstances, he still shares and identifies with our pain. You are not alone in it".

³³ When Jesus saw her weeping, and the Jews who had come along with her also weeping, he was deeply moved in spirit and troubled. ³⁵ Jesus wept.

John 11:33, 35

DAY 16

"His presence in our mess, takes every smell away. Just get Him involved".

³⁹ "Take away the stone," he said. "But, Lord," said Martha, the sister of the dead man, "by this time there is a bad odour, for he has been there four days." ⁴⁰ Then Jesus said, "Did I not tell you that if you believe, you will see the glory of God?"

John 11:39-40

DAY 17

"Only that which edifies, should be vocalized. Never waste your words, but use them wisely and rightly"

²⁹ Do not let any unwholesome talk come out of your mouths, but only what is helpful for building others up according to their needs, that it may benefit those who listen.

Ephesians 4:29

DAY 18

"Every situation and challenge around you, is an opportunity to replicate God where you are. Don't limit what he can do through you".

[19] Now the Lord God had formed out of the ground all the wild animals and all the birds in the sky. He brought them to the man to see what he would name them; and whatever the man called each living creature, that was its name.

Gen 2:19

DAY 19

"There is no loss for God that is not accompanied with gain from God. Just let it go".

²¹ So the Lord God caused the man to fall into a deep sleep; and while he was sleeping, he took one of the man's ribs[g] and then closed up the place with flesh. ²² Then the Lord God made a woman from the rib[h] he had taken out of the man, and he brought her to the man. ²³ The man said, "This is now bone of my bones and flesh of my flesh; she shall be called 'woman,' for she was taken out of man.

Gen 2:21-23.

DAY 20

"When God covers you, there is no shame. Run to Him for cover".

[25] *Adam and his wife were both naked, and they felt no shame.*

Genesis 2:25

DAY 21

"What you have or don't have does not define who you are, but having Jesus makes all the difference"

[15] Then he said to them, "Watch out! Be on your guard against all kinds of greed; life does not consist in an abundance of possessions."

Luke 12:15

DAY 22

"The bed you have, you need rest to sleep on it; the money you have, you need life to spend it; the house and the family you have, you need peace to live in it; and only Jesus gives all. Pursue him."

[15] Then he said to them, "Watch out! Be on your guard against all kinds of greed; life does not consist in an abundance of possessions.

Luke 12:15

DAY 23

"Nothing resists you that cannot be resisted, when heaven grants you victory. Just align with God".

[36] From Aroer on the rim of the Arnon Gorge, and from the town in the gorge, even as far as Gilead, not one town was too strong for us. The LORD our God gave us all of them.

Deuteronomy 2:36

DAY 24

"If it doesn't satisfy or edify, then it is not worth a single sacrifice. Quit worthless ventures, and pursue value only".

[2] Why spend money on what is not bread, and your labour on what does not satisfy? Listen, listen to me, and eat what is good, and you will delight in the richest of fare.

Isaiah 55:2

DAY 25

"When you give the devil a mile, he will go a thousand miles. Refuse him anyhow".

²⁷ and do not give the devil a foothold.

¹⁰ The thief comes only to steal and kill and destroy; I have come that they may have life, and have it to the full.

(Ephesians 4:27; John 10:10)

DAY 26

"What makes life miserable is not what we don't have, but often what we have and don't use. Be content and make the most of what you have".

[15] Then he said to them, "Watch out! Be on your guard against all kinds of greed; life does not consist in an abundance of possessions."

Luke 12:15

DAY 27

"The name of any man without Christ, is seemingly irrelevant to God. Get to know him, to be known by him"

¹⁶ And he told them this parable: "The ground of a certain rich man yielded an abundant harvest.

***(Luke 12:16).*he

DAY 28

"Your name and fame matter more to God, only when you are doing what matters in his kingdom. Get involved with what matters to him".

¹⁶ And he told them this parable: "The ground of a certain rich man yielded an abundant harvest.

(Luke 12:16).

DAY 29

"Because you are not everybody, you cannot afford to do what everybody is doing. You are somebody's, so do it His way".

¹⁵ For it is God's will that by doing well you should silence the ignorant talk of foolish people. ¹⁶ Live as free people, but do not use your freedom as a cover-up for evil; live as God's slaves.

1 Peter 2:15-16

DAY 30

"Don't be chained to your past, live not only in the present, but head towards a golden future".

[11] When I was a child, I talked like a child, I thought like a child, I reasoned like a child. When I became a man, I put the ways of childhood behind me. [12] For now we see only a reflection as in a mirror; then we shall see face to face. Now I know in part; then I shall know fully, even as I am fully known.

1 Corinthian 13:11

DAY 31

"His journey to the cross, marked the beginning of your journey to freedom. Whatever ties you down, He sets you free- so live free"

[24] *"He himself bore our sins" in his body on the cross, so that we might die to sins and live for righteousness; "by his wounds you have been healed."* [25] *For "you were like sheep going astray,"[a] but now you have returned to the Shepherd and Overseer of your souls.*

1 Peter 2:24-25

DAY 32

"You don't have to have it, to believe it. When He says it, He will do it. His words are yeah and amen".

⁴ "So he left the land of the Chaldeans and settled in Harran. After the death of his father, God sent him to this land where you are now living. ⁵ He gave him no inheritance here, not even enough ground to set his foot on. But God promised him that he and his descendants after him would possess the land, even though at that time Abraham had no child.

Acts 7:4-5

DAY 33

"If you wait to have the promise, to believe the promise, you may never believe the promise to see the promise come to pass. Just have faith".

⁴ "So he left the land of the Chaldeans and settled in Harran. After the death of his father, God sent him to this land where you are now living. ⁵ He gave him no inheritance here, not even enough ground to set his foot on. But God promised him that he and his descendants after him would possess the land, even though at that time Abraham had no child.

Acts 7:4-5

DAY 34

"Never step out in your own time, in the pursuit of his assignment, when it is not yet his time. It could be dangerous".

²³ "When Moses was forty years old, he decided to visit his own people, the Israelites. ²⁴ He saw one of them being mistreated by an Egyptian, so he went to his defence and avenged him by killing the Egyptian. ²⁵ Moses thought that his own people would realize that God was using him to rescue them, but they did not. ²⁶ The next day Moses came upon two Israelites who were fighting. He tried to reconcile them by saying, 'Men, you are brothers; why do you want to hurt each other?' ²⁷ "But the man who was mistreating the other pushed Moses aside and said, 'Who made you ruler and judge over us?

Acts 7:23-27

DAY 35

"When you allow time, it processes you well and equips you with the right mind-set for your assignment. Never step out in your own time".

²³ "When Moses was forty years old, he decided to visit his own people, the Israelites. ²⁴ He saw one of them being mistreated by an Egyptian, so he went to his defense and avenged him by killing the Egyptian. ²⁵ Moses thought that his own people would realize that God was using him to rescue them, but they did not. ²⁶ The next day Moses came upon two Israelites who were fighting. He tried to reconcile them by saying, 'Men, you are brothers; why do you want to hurt each other?' ²⁷ "But the man who was mistreating the other pushed Moses aside and said, 'Who made you ruler and judge over us? ²⁸ are you thinking of killing me as you killed the Egyptian yesterday?'[a] ²⁹ When Moses heard this, he fled to Midian, where he settled as a foreigner and had two sons.

(Acts 7:23-29).

DAY 36

"He will always bring you back to where and what you've been running away from-because you are an item in His agenda. Just stop running".

*1 The word of the LORD came to Jonah son of Amittai: ² "Go to the great city of Nineveh and preach against it, because its wickedness has come up before me." ³ But Jonah ran away from the LORD and headed for Tarshish. He went down to Joppa, where he found a ship bound for that port. After paying the fare, he went aboard and sailed for Tarshish to flee from the LORD. ¹⁷ Now the LORD provided a huge fish to swallow Jonah, and Jonah was in the belly of the fish three days and three nights. ²¹⁰ And the LORD commanded the fish, and it vomited Jonah onto dry land. **3** Then the word of the LORD came to Jonah a second time: ² "Go to the great city of Nineveh and proclaim to it the message I give you." ³ Jonah obeyed the word of the LORD and went to Nineveh. Now Nineveh was a very large city; it took three days to go through it. ⁴ Jonah began by going* *a day's journey into the city, proclaiming, "Forty more days and Nineveh will be overthrown."*

Acts 7:29-34.

²⁹ When Moses heard this, he fled to Midian, where he settled as a foreigner and had two sons. ³⁰ "After forty years had passed, an angel appeared to Moses in the flames of a burning bush in the desert near Mount Sinai. ³¹ When he saw this, he was amazed at the sight. As he went over to get a closer look, he heard the Lord say: ³² 'I am the God of your fathers, the God of Abraham, Isaac and Jacob.'[a] Moses trembled with fear and did not dare to look. ³³ "Then the Lord said to him, 'Take off your sandals, for the place where you are standing is holy ground. ³⁴ I have indeed seen the oppression of my people in Egypt. I have heard their groaning and have come down to set them free. Now come, I will send you back to Egypt.'[b]

Jonah 1: 1-3, 17; 2:10; 3:1-4; Acts 7:29-34).

DAY 37

"You don't have to physically go back to where you used to be, to be whom you used to be, but in your heart. Let the change begin from the heart".

39 "But our ancestors refused to obey him. Instead, they rejected him and in their hearts turned back to Egypt. 40 They told Aaron, 'Make us gods who will go before us. As for this fellow Moses who led us out of Egypt—we don't know what has happened to him!' 41 That was the time they made an idol in the form of a calf. They brought sacrifices to it and revealed in what their own hands had made.

Acts 7:39-41

DAY 38

"He despised the most precious and expensive edifice, just to live in you. What a wonderful piece of creation you are. Celebrate yourself every time, for His glory".

[48] "However, the Most High does not live in houses made by human hands. As the prophet says:

(Acts 7:48).

DAY 39

"Your connection with heaven, protects and secures everything connected to you. Connect and stay connected- it pays".

[10] Now there was a famine in the land, and Abram went down to Egypt to live there for a while because the famine was severe. [11] As he was about to enter Egypt, he said to his wife Sarai, "I know what a beautiful woman you are. [12] When the Egyptians see you, they will say, 'This is his wife.' Then they will kill me but will let you live. [13] Say you are my sister, so that I will be treated well for your sake and my life will be spared because of you." [14] When Abram came to Egypt, the Egyptians saw that Sarai was a very beautiful woman. [15] And when Pharaoh's officials saw her, they praised her to Pharaoh, and she was taken into his palace. [16] He treated Abram well for her sake, and Abram acquired sheep and cattle, male and female donkeys, male and female servants, and camels. [17] But the LORD

inflicted serious diseases on Pharaoh and his household because of Abram's wife Sarai. [18] So Pharaoh summoned Abram. "What have you done to me?" he said. "Why didn't you tell me she was your wife? [19] Why did you say, 'She is my sister,' so that I took her to be my wife? Now then, here is your wife. Take her and go!" [20] Then Pharaoh gave orders about Abram to his men, and they sent him on his way, with his wife and everything he had.

Gen 12:10-20

DAY 40

= *"If God is all you have, you will never loose what you have. Even if it seems lost, you'll always gain all you've had".*

[20] Then Pharaoh gave orders about Abram to his men, and they sent him on his way, with his wife and everything he had.

Gen 12:20

DAY 41

"Lives and places destined for greatness, are often plagued with vicissitudes. Don't quit yet, you will smile soon".

⁷ *The* LORD *appeared to Abram and said, "To your offspring[a] I will give this land." So he built an altar there to the* LORD*, who had appeared to him.*

¹⁰ *Now there was a famine in the land, and Abram went down to Egypt to live there for a while because the famine was severe.*

Gen 12:7, 10

DAY 42

"Because his (Devil) time is short, he speeds up his evil. Be watchful"

¹² Therefore rejoice, you heavens and you who dwell in them! But woe to the earth and the sea, because the devil has gone down to you! He is filled with fury, because he knows that his time is short."

Rev 12:12

DAY 43

"If the devil has got a plan for your life, what plan have you got for your life? I know of someone (Jesus) with a better plan for your life. Look up to him".

²⁵ In opposition to him these citizens of Shechem set men on the hilltops to ambush and rob everyone who passed by, and this was reported to Abimelek.

¹¹ For I know the plans I have for you," declares the LORD, "plans to prosper you and not to harm you, plans to give you hope and a future.

(Judges 9:25; Jeremiah 29:11).

DAY 44z

"When you honor God, He honors your words. Don't let your words fall to the ground. Just honor Him".

19 The LORD was with Samuel as he grew up, and he let none of Samuel's words fall to the ground

1 Samuel 3:19

DAY 45

"When you stay with the word, it keeps you from the world".

⁹ How can a young person stay on the path of purity? By living according to your word.

Psalm 119:9

DAY 46

"Before you ignore what is always present, be reminded, that it may not always be present. Don't ignore it".

³ how shall we escape if we ignore so great a salvation? This salvation, which was first announced by the Lord, was confirmed to us by those who heard him.

Heb 2:3

DAY 47

"Quit magnifying your struggle, and magnify what He did on the cross-then you will overcome".

[24] "He himself bore our sins" in his body on the cross, so that we might die to sins and live for righteousness; "by his wounds you have been healed."

1 Peter 2:24

DAY 48

"Kindness is a seed. Sow one".

³ *The king asked, "Is there no one still alive from the house of Saul to whom I can show God's kindness?" Ziba answered the king, "There is still a son of Jonathan; he is lame in both feet."* ⁷ *"Don't be afraid," David said to him, "for I will surely show you kindness for the sake of your father Jonathan. I will restore to you all the land that belonged to your grandfather Saul, and you will always eat at my table."* ⁹ *Then the chief cupbearer said to Pharaoh, "Today I am reminded of my shortcomings.* ¹⁰ *Pharaoh was once angry with his servants, and he imprisoned me and the chief baker in the house of the captain of the guard.* ¹¹ *Each of us had a dream the same night, and each dream had a meaning of its own.* ¹² *Now a young Hebrew was there with us, a servant of the captain of the guard. We told him our dreams, and he interpreted them for us, giving each man the interpretation of his dream.* ¹³ *And things turned out exactly as he interpreted them to us: I was restored to my position, and the other man was impaled."* ¹⁴ *So Pharaoh sent for Joseph, and he*

was quickly brought from the dungeon. When he had shaved and changed his clothes, he came before Pharaoh

2 Samuel 9:3-7; Gen 41:9-14

DAY 49

"You need just an encounter with kindness, for your story to change".

³ The king asked, "Is there no one still alive from the house of Saul to whom I can show God's kindness?" Ziba answered the king, "There is still a son of Jonathan; he is lame in both feet."

⁴ "Where is he?" the king asked. Ziba answered, "He is at the house of Makir son of Ammiel in Lo Debar."

⁷ "Don't be afraid," David said to him, "for I will surely show you kindness for the sake of your father Jonathan. I will restore to you all the land that belonged to your grandfather Saul, and you will always eat at my table."

⁸ Mephibosheth bowed down and said, "What is your servant, that you should notice a dead dog like me?"

2 Samuel 9:3

DAY 50

"When you lose sense of the value of his presence, you can't go far".

¹¹ Do not cast me from your presence or take your Holy Spirit from me.
¹² Restore to me the joy of your salvation and grant me a willing spirit, to sustain me. ¹³ Then I will teach transgressors your ways,
so that sinners will turn back to you.

Psalm 51:11-13

DAY 51

"To every giant, there is a giant against him or her. You need God to defeat your giant"

⁴ Sometime later, he fell in love with a woman in the Valley of Sorek whose name was Delilah. *⁵ The rulers of the Philistines went to her and said, "See if you can lure him into showing you the secret of his great strength and how we can overpower him so we may tie him up and subdue him. Each one of us will give you eleven hundred shekels[o] of silver."* ¹⁷ So he told her everything. "No razor has ever been used on my head," he said, "because I have been a Nazirite dedicated to God from my mother's womb. If my head were shaved, my strength would leave me, and I would become as weak as any other man." ¹⁸ When Delilah saw that he had told her everything, she sent word to the rulers of the Philistines, "Come back once more; he has told me everything." So the rulers of the Philistines returned with the silver in their hands. ¹⁹ After putting him to sleep on her lap, she called for someone to shave off the seven braids of his hair, and so began to subdue him.[a] And his strength left him. ²⁰ Then she called, "Samson, the Philistines are upon you!"

He awoke from his sleep and thought, "I'll go out as before and shake myself free." But he did not know that the Lord had left him.

Judges 16:4-5, 17-20

DAY 52

Protect your source. It's the only thing that the devil targets.

⁵ *The rulers of the Philistines went to her and said, "See if you can lure him into showing you the secret of his great strength and how we can overpower him so we may tie him up and subdue him. Each one of us will give you eleven hundred shekels[a] of silver."* ¹⁷ So he told her everything. "No razor has ever been used on my head," he said, "because I have been a Nazirite dedicated to God from my mother's womb. If my head were shaved, my strength would leave me, and I would become as weak as any other man." ¹⁸ When Delilah saw that he had told her everything, she sent word to the rulers of the Philistines, "Come back once more; he has told me everything." So the rulers of the Philistines returned with the silver in their hands. ¹⁹ After putting him to sleep on her lap, she called for someone to shave off the seven braids of his hair, and so began to subdue him.[a] And his strength left him. ²⁰ Then she called, "Samson, the Philistines are upon you!"

He awoke from his sleep and thought, "I'll go out as before and shake myself free." But he did not know that the LORD had left him.

Judges 16:5, 17-20

DAY 53

The devil goes for the sight first, when he strikes. It rubs you of revelation and honour. Protect it.

²¹ Then the Philistines seized him, gouged out his eyes and took him down to Gaza. Binding him with bronze shackles, they set him to grinding grain in the prison. ²² But the hair on his head began to grow again after it had been shaved.

²³ Now the rulers of the Philistines assembled to offer a great sacrifice to Dagon their god and to celebrate, saying, "Our god has delivered Samson, our enemy, into our hands." ²⁴ When the people saw him, they praised their god, saying, "Our god has delivered our enemy into our hands,
the one who laid waste our land and multiplied our slain."

²⁵ While they were in high spirits, they shouted, "Bring out Samson to entertain us." So they called Samson out of the prison, and he performed for them.

Judges 16:2-25

DAY 54

"The price you pay for the instructions you refuse, is often costly. Be watchful and teachable".

18 When Delilah saw that he had told her everything, she sent word to the rulers of the Philistines, "Come back once more; he has told me everything." So the rulers of the Philistines returned with the silver in their hands. *19* After putting him to sleep on her lap, she called for someone to shave off the seven braids of his hair, and so began to subdue him.[c] And his strength left him.

20 Then she called, "Samson, the Philistines are upon you!" He awoke from his sleep and thought, "I'll go out as before and shake myself free." But he did not know that the LORD had left him. *21* Then the Philistines seized him, gouged out his eyes and took him down to Gaza. Binding him with bronze shackles, they set him to grinding grain in *the prison.*

Judges 16:18-21

DAY 55

"You are not what you think, neither are you what you feel, but what he says you are".

⁹ But you are a chosen people, a royal priesthood, a holy nation, God's special possession, that you may declare the praises of him who called you out of darkness into his wonderful light.

1 peter 2:9

DAY 56

"When you choose not to choose, it's a choice. You better choose and choose right. The neutral ground is not always the best place to be".

¹⁵ *And if it seem evil unto you to serve the LORD, choose you this day whom ye will serve; whether the gods which your fathers served that were on the other side of the flood, or the gods of the Amorites, in whose land ye dwell: but as for me and my house, we will serve the LORD.*

Joshua 24:15

DAY 57

"When you amplify your circumstance, at the expense of what He has done for you, you limit Him from doing more and so much more for you".

⁵ Trust in the Lord with all your heart and lean not on your own understanding;
⁶ in all your ways submit to him, and he will make your paths straight.

Proverbs 3:5-6

DAY 58

"The devil is not joking with you, reducing you to a chaff of weed is his agenda. Watch it and never give him a chance".

31 "Simon, Simon, Satan has asked to sift all of you as wheat. 32 But I have prayed for you, Simon, that your faith may not fail. And when you have turned back, strengthen your brothers."

33 But he replied, "Lord, I am ready to go with you to prison and to death."

(Luke 22:31-33)

DAY 59

"The bigger the blessing, the bigger the opposition. Go for it fearlessly".

^{26} *They came back to Moses and Aaron and the whole Israelite community at Kadesh in the Desert of Paran. There they reported to them and to the whole assembly and showed them the fruit of the land.* ^{27} *They gave Moses this account: "We went into the land to which you sent us, and it does flow with milk and honey! Here is its fruit.* ^{28} *But the people who live there are powerful, and the cities are fortified and very large. We even saw descendants of Anak there.* ^{29} *The Amalekites live in the Negev; the Hittites, Jebusites and Amorites live in the hill country; and the Canaanites live near the sea and along the Jordan."*

^{30} *Then Caleb silenced the people before Moses and said, "We should go up and take possession of the land, for we can certainly do it."*

Number 13:26-30

DAY 60

"Amplify the size of your God, not the size of your opposition".

²⁹ *The Amalekites live in the Negev; the Hittites, Jebusites and Amorites live in the hill country; and the Canaanites live near the sea and along the Jordan."*

³⁰ *Then Caleb silenced the people before Moses and said, "We should go up and take possession of the land, for we can certainly do it."*

(Numbers 13:29-30).

DAY 61

"You will miss it and miss out, when you give up. Don't give up, still hold on".

^{30} Then Caleb silenced the people before Moses and said, "We should go up and take possession of the land, for we can certainly do it."

^{31} But the men who had gone up with him said, "We can't attack those people; they are stronger than we are." ^{32} And they spread among the Israelites a bad report about the land they had explored. They said, "The land we explored devours those living in it. All the people we saw there are of great size. ^{33} We saw the Nephilim there (the descendants of Anak come from the Nephilim). We seemed like grasshoppers in our own eyes, and we looked the same to them." **Numbers 13:30-33**

DAY 62

"The secret of staying in charge in life, is giving God charge over your life. Don't miss out on this".

² The LORD was with Joseph so that he prospered, and he lived in the house of his Egyptian master. ⁵ From the time he put him in charge of his household and of all that he owned, the LORD blessed the household of the Egyptian because of Joseph. The blessing of the LORD was on everything Potiphar had, both in the house and in the field

²¹ the LORD was with him; he showed him kindness and granted him favour in the eyes of the prison warden. ²² So the warden put Joseph in charge of all those held in the prison, and he was made responsible for all that was done there.

⁴¹ So Pharaoh said to Joseph, "I hereby put you in charge of the whole land of Egypt."

Gen 39:2, 5, 21-22; Gen 41:41

DAY 63

"We sometimes suffer for the wrong things in life. What a gainless pain. Let your suffering be for a worthy cause always"

[16] However, if you suffer as a Christian, do not be ashamed, but praise God that you bear that name. [17] For it is time for judgment to begin with God's household; and if it begins with us, what will the outcome be for those who do not obey the gospel of God?

1 peter 4:16-17

DAY 64

"If you settle at the junction where you only need to pass through, you could end there. Move on, don't settle".

[31] Terah took his son Abram, his grandson Lot son of Haran, and his daughter-in-law Sarai, the wife of his son Abram, and together they set out from Ur of the Chaldeans to go to Canaan. But when they came to Harran, they settled there.

[32] Terah lived 205 years, and he died in Harran.

Gen 11:31-32

DAY 65

"When He makes, no one can unmake. Just allow Him to make you".

[2] "I will make you into a great nation, and I will bless you; I will make your name great, and you will be a blessing.

Gen 12:2

DAY 66

"Your connection with the main source, blesses everyone connected to you. Stay connected".

⁵ Now Lot, who was moving about with Abram, also had flocks and herds and tents. ⁶ But the land could not support them while they stayed together, for their possessions were so great that they were not able to stay together

Gen 13:5-6

DAY 67

"When you insist on having more than your share today, hardly can you escape sharing your glory tomorrow. Don't be greedy".

²² But Abram said to the king of Sodom, "With raised hand I have sworn an oath to the Lord, God Most High, Creator of heaven and earth, ²³ that I will accept nothing belonging to you, not even a thread or the strap of a sandal, so that you will never be able to say, 'I made Abram rich.' ²⁴ I will accept nothing but what my men have eaten and the share that belongs to the men who went with me—to Aner, Eshkol and Mamre. Let them have their share."

Gen 14:22-24

DAY 68

"The price you pay for trying to help God, often supersedes what you pay for waiting for Him instead. Just wait, it pays more".

16 Now Sarai, Abram's wife had borne him no children, and she had an Egyptian maid whose name was Hagar. ² So Sarai said to Abram, "Now behold, the Lord has prevented me from bearing children. Please go in to my maid; perhaps I will obtain children through her." And Abram listened to the voice of Sarai. ³ After Abram had lived ten years in the land of Canaan, Abram's wife Sarai took Hagar the Egyptian, her maid, and gave her to her husband Abram as his wife. ⁴ He went in to Hagar, and she conceived; and when she saw that she had conceived, her mistress was despised in her sight. ⁵ And Sarai said to Abram, "May the wrong done me be upon you. I gave my maid into your [c]arms, but when she saw that she had conceived, I was despised in her sight. May the Lord judge between you and me."

Gen 16:1-5

DAY 69

When He answers it for you, you will always have no case to answer. Leave it to Him to answer for you.

[17] But beware of men, for they will hand you over to the courts and scourge you in their synagogues; [18] and you will even be brought before governors and kings for my sake, as a testimony to them and to the Gentiles. [19] But when they hand you over, do not worry about how or what you are to say; for it will be given you in that hour what you are to say. [20] For it is not you who speak, but it is the Spirit of your Father who speaks in you

Matthew 10:17-20

DAY 70

"You need something more than life, to survive life. Jesus is the Life you need"

1 In the beginning was the Word, and the Word was with God, and the Word was God. ² He was with God in the beginning. ³ Through him all things were made; without him nothing was made that has been made. ⁴ In him was life, and that life was the light of all mankind. ⁵ The light shines in the darkness, and the darkness has not overcome[a] it.

John 1:1-5

DAY 71

"The fruit that comes with trying to help God is not always sweet. Wait for His time".

Now Sarai, Abram's wife, had borne him no children. But she had an Egyptian slave named Hagar; ² so she said to Abram, "The LORD has kept me from having children. Go, sleep with my slave; perhaps I can build a family through her." Abram agreed to what Sarai said. ³ So after Abram had been living in Canaan ten years, Sarai his wife took her Egyptian slave Hagar and gave her to her husband to be his wife. ⁴ He slept with Hagar, and she conceived. When she knew she was pregnant, she began to despise her mistress. ⁵ Then Sarai said to Abram, "You are responsible for the wrong I am suffering. I put my slave in your arms, and now that she knows she is pregnant, she despises me. May the LORD judge between you and me?"

Gen 19:36-38; 16:1-5

DAY 72

"Your connection with divinity, insures everything connected to you. Stay connected, it's the best insurance policy".

² and there Abraham said of his wife Sarah, "She is my sister." Then Abimelek king of Gerar sent for Sarah and took her.

³ But God came to Abimelek in a dream one night and said to him, "You are as good as dead because of the woman you have taken; she is a married woman."

Genesis 20:2-3

DAY 73

"Whatever God respects, He protects- don't play with it, rather take it serious".

Now Abraham moved on from there into the region of the Negev and lived between Kadesh and Shur. For a while he stayed in Gerar, [2] and there Abraham said of his wife Sarah, "She is my sister." Then Abimelek king of Gerar sent for Sarah and took her. [3] But God came to Abimelek in a dream one night and said to him, "You are as good as dead because of the woman you have taken; she is a married woman." [4] Now Abimelek had not gone near her, so he said, "Lord, will you destroy an innocent nation? [5] Did he not say to me, 'She is my sister,' and didn't she also say, 'He is my brother'? I have done this with a clear conscience and clean hands." [6] Then God said to him in the dream, "Yes, I know you did this with a clear conscience, and so I have kept you from sinning against me. That is why I did not let you touch her.

Gen 20:1-6

DAY 74

"Obedience is costly, but it's worth it. Just try it and see".

⁴ I will make your descendants as numerous as the stars in the sky and will give them all these lands, and through your offspring[a] all nations on earth will be blessed,[b] ⁵ because Abraham obeyed me and did everything I required of him, keeping my commands, my decrees and my instructions." ⁶ So Isaac stayed in Gerar.

Gen 26:4-6

DAY 75

"When you take side with God, your life attracts your world and even silences your enemies. Do just that".

²⁸ They answered, "We saw clearly that the LORD was with you; so we said, 'There ought to be a sworn agreement between us'—between us and you. Let us make a treaty with you

Gen 26:28

DAY 76

"What do you do, when the current experience does not match the future promise? Just wait."

¹⁵ *"Do not touch my anointed ones; do my prophets no harm."* ¹⁶ *He called down famine on the land and destroyed all their supplies of food;*
¹⁷ *and he sent a man before them— Joseph, sold as a slave.*
¹⁸ *They bruised his feet with shackles, his neck was put in irons,*
¹⁹ *till what he foretold came to pass, till the word of the LORD proved him true.* ²⁰ *The king sent and released him, the ruler of peoples set him free.*

Psalm 105:15-20

DAY 77

"Go beyond just the acts into knowing his ways".

⁷ He made known his ways to Moses, his deeds to the people of Israel:

Psalm 103:7

DAY 78

"His ways will show you the acts- go beyond just pursuing the acts".

7 He made known his ways to Moses, his deeds to the people of Israel:

Psalm 103:7

DAY 79

"What dominates your heart, determines your pursuits".

¹ As the deer pants for streams of water, so my soul pants for you, my God.
² My soul thirsts for God, for the living God. When can I go and meet with God?

Psalm 42:1-2

DAY 80

"Even if it will cost you, whatever the cost might be; his presence is the place to be".

¹ *Keep me safe, my God, for in you I take refuge.*

² *I say to the LORD, "You are my Lord; apart from you I have no good thing."* ³ *I say of the holy people who are in the land, "They are the noble ones in whom is all my delight."* ⁴ *Those who run after other gods will suffer more and more. I will not pour out libations of blood to such gods or take up their names on my lips.* ⁵ *LORD, you alone are my portion and my cup;*
you make my lot secure. **Psalm 16:16**

DAY 81

Whatever you have, that could have God from you, let God have it from you.

Sometime later God tested Abraham. He said to him, "Abraham!"

"Here I am," he replied. ² Then God said, "Take your son, your only son, whom you love—Isaac—and go to the region of Moriah. Sacrifice him there as a burnt offering on a mountain I will show you." ³ Early the next morning Abraham got up and loaded his donkey. He took with him two of his servants and his son Isaac. When he had cut enough wood for the burnt offering, he set out for the place God had told him about. ⁴ On the third day Abraham looked up and saw the place in the distance. ⁵ He said to his servants, "Stay here with the donkey while I and the boy go over there. We will worship and then we will come back to you." ⁶ Abraham took the wood for the burnt offering and placed it on his son Isaac, and he himself

carried the fire and the knife. As the two of them went on together, [7] Isaac spoke up and said to his father Abraham, "Father?" "Yes, my son?" Abraham replied. "The fire and wood are here," Isaac said, "but where is the lamb for the burnt offering?" [8] Abraham answered, "God himself will provide the lamb for the burnt offering, my son." And the two of them went on together. [9] When they reached the place God had told him about, Abraham built an altar there and arranged the wood on it. He bound his son Isaac and laid him on the altar, on top of the wood.

Gen 22:1-9

DAY 82

"When your pursuits in life are not aligned with purpose- you will compromise invaluable pursuits for worthless activities".

8 As Jesus and his disciples were on their way, he came to a village where a woman named Martha opened her home to him. 39 She had a sister called Mary, who sat at the Lord's feet listening to what he said. 40 But Martha was distracted by all the preparations that had to be made. She came to him and asked, "Lord, don't you care that my sister has left me to do the work by myself? Tell her to help me!" 41 "Martha, Martha," the Lord answered, "you are worried and upset about many things, 42 but few things are needed—or indeed only one.[a] Mary has chosen what is better, and it will not be taken away from her."

Luke 10:38-42

DAY 83

"When you quench it from within, it reflects on the outside. Let your light shine and keep it burning".

35 See to it, then, that the light within you is not darkness. 36 Therefore, if your whole body is full of light, and no part of it dark, it will be just as full of light as when a lamp shines its light on you."

Luke 11:35-36

DAY 84

"When you quit making the main thing the main thing in your life, you will spend the rest of your life making the minor things the main thing in your life. Measure in major not minor".

13 Someone in the crowd said to him, "Teacher, tell my brother to divide the inheritance with me." 14 Jesus replied, "Man, who appointed me a judge or an arbiter between you?" 15 Then he said to them, "Watch out! Be on your guard against all kinds of greed; life does not consist in an abundance of possessions."

16 And he told them this parable: "The ground of a certain rich man yielded an abundant harvest. 17 He thought to himself, 'What shall I do? I have no place to store my crops.' 18 "Then he said, 'This is what I'll do. I will tear down my barns and build bigger ones, and there I will store my surplus grain. 19 And I'll say to myself, "You have plenty of grain laid up for many years. Take life easy; eat, drink and be merry."'

20 "But God said to him, 'You fool! This very night your life will be demanded from you. Then who will get what you have prepared for yourself?'

21 "This is how it will be with whoever stores up things for themselves but is not rich toward God."

Luke 12:13-21

DAY 85

"If the minor requirement for survival supersedes your ability, then why worry about the major. Just let God in all".

25 Who of you by worrying can add a single hour to your life[a]? 26 Since you cannot do this very little thing, why do you worry about the rest?

27 "Consider how the wild flowers grow. They do not labour or spin. Yet I tell you, not even Solomon in all his splendour was dressed like one of these. 28 If that is how God clothes the grass of the field, which is here today, and tomorrow is thrown into the fire, how much more will he clothe you—you of little faith!

Luke12-25-28

DAY 86

"If you wait for your productivity to be questioned, before you bear fruit, it may be your last chance. Just do something".

6 Then he told this parable: "A man had a fig tree growing in his vineyard, and he went to look for fruit on it but did not find any. 7 So he said to the man who took care of the vineyard, 'For three years now I've been coming to look for fruit on this fig tree and haven't found any. Cut it down! Why should it use up the soil?'

8 "'Sir,' the man replied, 'leave it alone for one more year, and I'll dig around it and fertilize it. 9 If it bears fruit next year, fine! If not, then cut it down.'"

Luke 13:6-9

DAY 87

"Focusing on others as the main problem of your life, shields you from seeing the main problem in your life. Look within, you could be it".

5 You hypocrite, first take the plank out of your own eye, and then you will see clearly to remove the speck from your brother's eye.

Matthew 7:5

DAY 88

"The very you that God knows, may be the you, that you've never met. Get to meet God, to know more of you".

*5 "Before I formed you in the womb I knew[a] you,
before you were born I set you apart;
I appointed you as a prophet to the nations."*

Jeremiah 1:5

DAY 89

"Refusing his invitation robs you of your place at the banquet. Reserve your place with the invitation".

23 "Then the master told his servant, 'Go out to the roads and country lanes and compel them to come in, so that my house will be full. 24 I tell you, not one of those who were invited will get a taste of my banquet.'"

Luke 14:23-24

DAY 90

"When you hook-up with God, he will clutch the wheel of your enemies from reaching you. Hook to him".

24 During the last watch of the night the Lord looked down from the pillar of fire and cloud at the Egyptian army and threw it into confusion. 25 He jammed[a] the wheels of their chariots so that they had difficulty driving. And the Egyptians said, "Let's get away from the Israelites! The Lord is fighting for them against Egypt."

Exodus 14:24-25

DAY 91

"He will not necessarily bring you out of it, but will always be with you in it. Hold on some more".

8 Three times I pleaded with the Lord to take it away from me. 9 But he said to me, "My grace is sufficient for you, for my power is made perfect in weakness." Therefore I will boast all the more gladly about my weaknesses, so that Christ's power may rest on me.

2 Corinthians 12:8-9

DAY 92

"Why an alliance with him (Devil) - who questions every good thing coming your way? Just let him go".

10 On a Sabbath Jesus was teaching in one of the synagogues, 11 and a woman was there who had been crippled by a spirit for eighteen years. She was bent over and could not straighten up at all. 12 When Jesus saw her, he called her forward and said to her, "Woman, you are set free from your infirmity." 13 Then he put his hands on her, and immediately she straightened up and praised God. 14 Indignant because Jesus had healed on the Sabbath, the synagogue leader said to the people, "There are six days for work. So come and be healed on those days, not on the Sabbath."

15 The Lord answered him, "You hypocrites! Doesn't each of you on the Sabbath untie your ox or donkey from the stall and lead it out to give it water? 16 Then should not this woman, a daughter of Abraham, whom Satan has kept bound for eighteen long years, be set free on the Sabbath day from what bound her?" 17 When he said this, all his opponents were humiliated, but the people were delighted with all the wonderful things he was doing.

Luke 13:10-17

DAY 93

"The little extra mile you are willing to go for him, could attract a little extra for you, from him. Even when you don't have to, go the extra mile".

44 Then he turned toward the woman and said to Simon, "Do you see this woman? I came into your house. You did not give me any water for my feet, but she wet my feet with her tears and wiped them with her hair. 45 You did not give me a kiss, but this woman, from the time I entered, has not stopped kissing my feet. 46 You did not put oil on my head, but she has poured perfume on my feet. 47 Therefore, I tell you, her many sins have been forgiven—as her great love has shown. But whoever has been forgiven little loves little."

Luke 7:44-47

DAY 94

"You can teach what you know, but can only reproduce who you are. Who are you?"

15 One day the evil spirit answered them, "Jesus I know, and Paul I know about, but who are you?"

Acts 19:15

DAY 95

"When you hold tight to old things, your hand can't be free to receive the new things awaiting you. Just let it go".

18 "Forget the former things; do not dwell on the past. 19 See, I am doing a new thing! Now it springs up; do you not perceive it? I am making a way in the wilderness and streams in the wasteland.

Isaiah 43:18-19

DAY 96

"How far he allows you go with him; depends on how much you believe in him. Don't doubt him, if you must get far with him".

49 While Jesus was still speaking, someone came from the house of Jairus, the synagogue leader. "Your daughter is dead," he said. "Don't bother the teacher anymore." 50 Hearing this, Jesus said to Jairus, "Don't be afraid; just believe, and she will be healed." 51 When he arrived at the house of Jairus, he did not let anyone go in with him except Peter, John and James, and the child's father and mother. 52 Meanwhile, all the people were wailing and mourning for her. "Stop wailing," Jesus said. "She is not dead but asleep." 53 They laughed at him, knowing that she was dead. 54 But he took her by the hand and said, "My child, get up!" 55 Her spirit returned, and at once she stood up. Then Jesus told them to give her something to eat. 56 Her parents were astonished, but he ordered them not to tell anyone what had happened.

Luke 8:49-56

DAY 97

"He loves you the way you are, but hates and frowns at you remaining where you are-the way you are. Grow some more".

6 Therefore let us move beyond the elementary teachings about Christ and be taken forward to maturity, not laying again the foundation of repentance from acts that lead to death,[a] and of faith in God,

Hebrews 6:1

DAY 98

"Until you put away what inhibits growth in your life, your age doesn't matter, you are still childish. Put it away".

11 When I was a child, I talked like a child, I thought like a child, I reasoned like a child. When I became a man, I put the ways of childhood behind me.

1corinthians 13:11

DAY 99

"When your priority in life is not in line with purpose, then your essence for living could be on the line also"

19 If only for this life we have hope in Christ, we are of all people most to be pitied.

1 Corinthians 15:19

DAY 100

"When you have God, you have it all. Pursue God".

2 fixing our eyes on Jesus, the pioneer and perfecter of faith. For the joy set before him he endured the cross, scorning its shame, and sat down at the right hand of the throne of God.

Heb 12:2

DAY 101

"If you worry, you die, when you don't worry, you still die; so why worry then? Just trust and seek God".

25 Who of you by worrying can add a single hour to your life[a]? 26 Since you cannot do this very little thing, why do you worry about the rest?

27 "Consider how the wild flowers grow. They do not labor or spin. Yet I tell you, not even Solomon in all his splendor was dressed like one of these. 28 If that is how God clothes the grass of the field, which is here today, and tomorrow is thrown into the fire, how much more will he clothe you—you of little faith! 29 And do not set your heart on what you will eat or drink; do not worry about it. 30 For the pagan world runs after all such things, and your Father knows that you need them. 31 But seek his kingdom, and these things will be given to you as well.

Luke 12:25-31

DAY 102

"Only by keeping to the principles, can your residency be guaranteed in the kingdom (Heaven)".

21 "Not everyone who says to me, 'Lord, Lord,' will enter the kingdom of heaven, but only the one who does the will of my Father who is in heaven

16 For the wise, like the fool, will not be long remembered; the days have already come when both have been forgotten. Like the fool, the wise too must die!

Matthew 7:21; Eccl 2:16

DAY 103

"The absence of the fruit compromises your purpose and limits your existence. Produce some fruits".

19 Every tree that does not bear good fruit is cut down and thrown into the fire

Matthew 7:19

DAY 104

"Never crave having from others what you can't give them back in return. As you would want done to you, do to others".

31 Do to others as you would have them do to you.

Luke 6:31

DAY 105

"Quit doing church and start doing God. Let Him be at the centre of it all".

13 The Lord says: "These people come near to me with their mouth and honour me with their lips, but their hearts are far from me. Their worship of me is based on merely human rules they have been taught.

Isaiah 29:13

DAY 106

"Every day in a man's life, is a bonus and a privilege. Don't joke with it, maximize it instead".

26 Otherwise Christ would have had to suffer many times since the creation of the world. But he has appeared once for all at the culmination of the ages to do away with sin by the sacrifice of himself. 27 Just as people are destined to die once, and after that to face judgment,

Heb 9:26-27

DAY 107

"Hardly would you escape struggling, when you trust your ability at the expense of God's grace. Just depend on him".

5 circumcised on the eighth day, of the people of Israel, of the tribe of Benjamin, a Hebrew of Hebrews; in regard to the law, a Pharisee; 6 as for zeal, persecuting the church; as for righteousness based on the law, faultless.

7 But whatever were gains to me I now consider loss for the sake of Christ. 8 What is more, I consider everything a loss because of the surpassing worth of knowing Christ Jesus my Lord, for whose sake I have lost all things. I consider them garbage, that I may gain Christ 9 and be found in him, not having a righteousness of my own that comes from the law, but that which is through faith in[a] Christ—the righteousness that comes from God on the basis of faith. 10 I want to know Christ—yes, to know the

power of his resurrection and participation in his sufferings, becoming like him in his death, 11 and so, somehow, attaining to the resurrection from the dead.
Phil 3:5-11

DAY 108

"Whatever takes the centre stage in your life, at the expense of the giver of life, is a god in your life. trust and boast in him alone".

5 circumcised on the eighth day, of the people of Israel, of the tribe of Benjamin, a Hebrew of Hebrews; in regard to the law, a Pharisee; 6 as for zeal, persecuting the church; as for righteousness based on the law, faultless.

7 But whatever were gains to me I now consider loss for the sake of Christ. 8 What is more, I consider everything a loss because of the surpassing worth of knowing Christ Jesus my Lord, for whose sake I have lost all things. I consider them garbage, that I may gain Christ 9 and be found in him, not having a righteousness of my own that comes from the law, but that which is through faith in[a] Christ—the righteousness that comes from God on the basis of faith. 10 I want to know Christ—yes, to know the

power of his resurrection and participation in his sufferings, becoming like him in his death, 11 and so, somehow, attaining to the resurrection from the dead.
Phil 3:5-11

DAY 109

"when you have a picture of the future, current struggles will not deter you. see beyond the present".

Do not turn me over to the desire of my foes,
for false witnesses rise up against me,
spouting malicious accusations.

13 I remain confident of this:
I will see the goodness of the Lord
in the land of the living.
14 Wait for the Lord;
be strong and take heart
and wait for the Lord.

Psalms 27:12-14

DAY 110

"Nothing qualifies a man for the best of God, other than the very best that God has done for man".

16 For God so loved the world that he gave his one and only Son, that whoever believes in him shall not perish but have eternal life. 6 All of us have become like one who is unclean, and all our righteous acts are like filthy rags; we all shrivel up like a leaf, and like the wind our sins sweep us away. 7 No one calls on your name or strives to lay hold of you; for you have hidden your face from us and have given us over to[a] our sins

John 3:16; Isaiah 64:6-7

DAY 111

"He never allows pain without a corresponding future and a promise. Just wait still"

7 "Before she goes into labor, she gives birth; before the pains come upon her, she delivers a son. 8 Who has ever heard of such things? Who has ever seen things like this? Can a country be born in a day or a nation be brought forth in a moment? Yet no sooner is Zion in labor than she gives birth to her children

Isaiah 66:7-8

DAY 112

"If you are waiting for a very correct person to correct you, before you get corrected, you may never be corrected. Everyone has some fault. Be teachable".

6 because the Lord disciplines the one he loves, and he chastens everyone he accepts as his son.

Heb 12:6

DAY 113

"If people would have to think twice, before correcting you, you could miss the best of opportunities to be a better person. Don't be tired of correction".

11 No discipline seems pleasant at the time, but painful. Later on, however, it produces a harvest of righteousness and peace for those who have been trained by it.

Heb 12:11

DAY 114

"The importance you attach to it, determines the effort you put on it. If you want it so much, go for it and wait some more".

4 *"For some time he refused. But finally he said to himself, 'Even though I don't fear God or care what people think, 5 yet because this widow keeps bothering me, I will see that she gets justice, so that she won't eventually come and attack me!'" 6 And the Lord said, "Listen to what the unjust judge says.*

Luke 18:4-6

DAY 115

"Until what tires you gets tired, you could still be worn out. Make up your mind not to be tired"

4 "For some time he refused. But finally he said to himself, 'Even though I don't fear God or care what people think, 5 yet because this widow keeps bothering me, I will see that she gets justice, so that she won't eventually come and attack me!'" 6 And the Lord said, "Listen to what the unjust judge says.

Luke 18:4-6

DAY 116

"Not always far from where you are, but so close are your enemies. Watch out and pray".

36 a man's enemies will be the members of his own household.'[a] 6 For a son dishonours his father, a daughter rises up against her mother, a daughter-in-law against her mother-in-law—a man's enemies are the members of his own household.

Mathew 10:36; Micah 7:6

DAY 117

"Not even your household, but God alone can be trusted. Trust Him more".

36 a man's enemies will be the members of his own household.'[a]

6 For a son dishonors his father, a daughter rises up against her mother, a daughter-in-law against her mother-in-law—a man's enemies are the members of his own household.

Mathew 10:36; Micah 7:6

DAY 118

"Waiting comes at a price, but it pays much more in the end. Just wait".

14 Wait for the Lord; be strong and take heart and wait for the Lord.

Psalm 27:14

DAY 119

"It costs to wait, but it pays to wait. Just wait when you have to"

14 Wait for the Lord; be strong and take heart and wait for the Lord.

Psalm 27:14

DAY 120

"In the day of adversity, how long you stand, depends on where you stand and who you stand with. Stand and stay with God".

5 For in the day of trouble he will keep me safe in his dwelling; he will hide me in the shelter of his sacred tent and set me high upon a rock. 6 Then my head will be exalted above the enemies who surround me; at his sacred tent I will sacrifice with shouts of joy; I will sing and make music to the Lord.

Psalm 27:5-6

DAY 121

"You can't be like God without God. Hold unto God to be like God"

5 "I am the vine; you are the branches. If you remain in me and I in you, you will bear much fruit; apart from me you can do nothing. 6 If you do not remain in me, you are like a branch that is thrown away and withers; such branches are picked up, thrown into the fire and burned. 7 If you remain in me and my words remain in you, ask whatever you wish, and it will be done for you.

John 15:5-7

DAY 122

"It's beyond words. Until you do wisdom, you have no wisdom".

19 The Son of Man came eating and drinking, and they say, 'Here is a glutton and a drunkard, a friend of tax collectors and sinners.' But wisdom is proved right by her deeds."

Mathew 11:19b

DAY 123

"If the Lord is your portion in life, you need no other portion to have enough in life. Just depend on Him".

After this, the word of the Lord came to Abram in a vision: "Do not be afraid, Abram. I am your shield, your very great reward.

5 He took him outside and said, "Look up at the sky and count the stars—if indeed you can count them." Then he said to him, "So shall your offspring be."

Gen 15:1, 5

DAY 124

"Wisdom is a key and an access code for influence. Ask God for it".

19 Wisdom makes one wise person more powerful than ten rulers in a city

Eccl 7:19

DAY 125

"The fear of God is an escape route from every snare of the enemy. Fear God".

26 I find more bitter than death the woman who is a snare, whose heart is a trap and whose hands are chains. The man who pleases God will escape her, but the sinner she will ensnare

Eccl 7:26

DAY 126

"Only death robs hope- for where there is life, there is hope. Quit quitting".

4 Anyone who is among the living has hope—even a live dog is better off than a dead lion!

Eccl 9:4

DAY 127

"It could be more confrontational when you walk away from confrontation, than staying calm when confronted. Be calm".

4 If a ruler's anger rises against you, do not leave your post; calmness can lay great offenses to rest.

Eccl 10:4

DAY 128

"When you have wisdom and fear not God, then you haven't begun yet".

13 Now all has been heard; here is the conclusion of the matter: Fear God and keep his commandments, for this is the duty of all mankind.

Eccl 12:13

DAY 129

"Even within the camp of your enemies- God can still raise a helper of destiny for you. Don't quit God".

19 Saul told his son Jonathan and all the attendants to kill David. But Jonathan had taken a great liking to David 2 and warned him, "My father Saul is looking for a chance to kill you. Be on your guard tomorrow morning; go into hiding and stay there. 3 I will go out and stand with my father in the field where you are. I'll speak to him about you and will tell you what I find out."

4 Jonathan spoke well of David to Saul his father and said to him, "Let not the king do wrong to his servant David; he has not wronged you, and what he has done has benefited you greatly. 5 He took his life in his hands when he killed the Philistine. The Lord won a great victory for all Israel, and you saw it and were glad. Why then would you do wrong to an innocent man like David by killing him for no reason?"

1samuel 19:1-5

DAY 130

"If it's a good thing, continue doing it until you die. The reward will outlast you"

9 Let us not become weary in doing good, for at the proper time we will reap a harvest if we do not give up.

Gal 6:9

DAY 131

"You will never pray differently or beyond where you are, until you grow discontented and tired of where you are".

9 Jabez was more honourable than his brothers. His mother had named him Jabez, saying, "I gave birth to him in pain." 10 Jabez cried out to the God of Israel, "Oh, that you would bless me and enlarge my territory! Let your hand be with me, and keep me from harm so that I will be free from pain." And God granted his request.

1 Chronicles 4:9-10

DAY 132

"Until you see yourself more than where you are, you will not pray your way out of where you are. Just know that- you are more than where you are".

9 Jabez was more honourable than his brothers. His mother had named him Jabez, saying, "I gave birth to him in pain." 10 Jabez cried out to the God of Israel, "Oh, that you would bless me and enlarge my territory! Let your hand be with me, and keep me from harm so that I will be free from pain." And God granted his request.

1 Chronicles 4:9-10

DAY 133

"You abuse the real you and discredit your maker, when you try to copy someone else. Stay YOU, you are wonderfully made"

14 I praise you because I am fearfully and wonderfully made; your works are wonderful, I know that full well.

Psalms 139:14

DAY 134

"Total dependence on God makes heroes of ordinary men. Depend on Him".

9 Jabez was more honourable than his brothers. His mother had named him Jabez,[a] saying, "I gave birth to him in pain." 10 Jabez cried out to the God of Israel, "Oh, that you would bless me and enlarge my territory! Let your hand be with me, and keep me from harm so that I will be free from pain." And God granted his request.

1 Chronicles 4:9-10.

DAY 135

"Nothing overshadows a man whose life is already being overshadowed by God. Let God overshadow you, it is the key to victory".

8 Were not the Cushites[a] and Libyans a mighty army with great numbers of chariots and horsemen[b]? Yet when you relied on the Lord, he delivered them into your hand.

2 Chronicles 16:8

DAY 136

"When He overshadows you, you operate far beyond the reach of your enemies. Just allow Him for a moment, if not a life time. You wouldn't regret It".

8 Were not the Cushites and Libyans a mighty army with great numbers of chariots and horsemen[c]? Yet when you relied on the Lord, he delivered them into your hand.

2Chonicles 16:8

DAY 137

"Negotiating with the devil, will not help you as much as resisting the devil. Resist him".

7 Submit yourselves, then, to God. Resist the devil, and he will flee from you.

James 4:7

DAY 138

"When you don't sense that something could be wrong sometimes, then everything is possibly wrong most times"

12 So, if you think you are standing firm, be careful that you don't fall!

1 Corinthians 10:12

DAY 139

"The greatest danger is not always being in a dangerous place, but being unwatchful in a dangerous place. Watch and pray".

36 Then Jesus went with his disciples to a place called Gethsemane, and he said to them, "Sit here while I go over there and pray."

38 Then he said to them, "My soul is overwhelmed with sorrow to the point of death. Stay here and keep watch with me."

41 "Watch and pray so that you will not fall into temptation. The spirit is willing, but the flesh is weak."

Mathew 26:36, 38, 41

DAY 140

"The devil is not your mate, only when you align with God are you his senior. Don't joke with any of His items".

19 If you belonged to the world, it would love you as its own. As it is, you do not belong to the world, but I have chosen you out of the world. That is why the world hates you.

John 15:19

DAY 141

"Only in an alliance with God is the devil a defeated liar. Just align with God".

10 The thief comes only to steal and kill and destroy; I have come that they may have life, and have it to the full.

John 10:10

DAY 142

"He is after you, because of who is in you. The one that lives in you is greater than the one that is against you. Refuse him, and he will flee".

7 Submit yourselves, then, to God. Resist the devil, and he will flee from you. 8 Come near to God and he will come near to you. Wash your hands, you sinners, and purify your hearts, you double-minded.

James 4:7-8

DAY 143

"When you quit the real source, you can't escape being weary. Stay connected".

5 "I am the vine; you are the branches. If you remain in me and I in you, you will bear much fruit; apart from me you can do nothing.

John 15:5

DAY 144

"You can let go everything, but don't let God go. Else, you could go down badly"

5 *"I am the vine; you are the branches. If you remain in me and I in you, you will bear much fruit; apart from me you can do nothing.*

John 15:5

DAY 145

"When you quit waiting on God, you will wait for other things for too long. Just wait some more".

13 I remain confident of this: I will see the goodness of the Lord in the land of the living. 14 Wait for the Lord; be strong and take heart and wait for the Lord

Psalm 27:13-14

DAY 146

"When you choose to connect with everything but God, you disconnect yourself from everything that counts".

2 fixing our eyes on Jesus, the pioneer and perfecter of faith. For the joy set before him he endured the cross, scorning its shame, and sat down at the right hand of the throne of God

Heb 12:2

30 "Woe to the obstinate children," declares the Lord, "to those who carry out plans that are not mine, forming an alliance, but not by my Spirit, heaping sin upon sin; 2 who go down to Egypt without consulting me; who look for help to Pharaoh's protection, to Egypt's shade for refuge. 3 But Pharaoh's protection will be to your shame, Egypt's shade will bring you disgrace.

Isaiah 30:1-3

DAY 147

"When you wait on the lord whilst waiting for whatever you are waiting for, it shortens your waiting time. Do wait on him".

63 He went out to the field one evening to meditate,[a] and as he looked up, he saw camels approaching. 64 Rebekah also looked up and saw Isaac. She got down from her camel 65 and asked the servant, "Who is that man in the field coming to meet us?"

"He is my master," the servant answered. So she took her veil and covered herself.

66 Then the servant told Isaac all he had done. 67 Isaac brought her into the tent of his mother Sarah, and he married Rebekah. So she became his wife, and he loved her; and Isaac was comforted after his mother's death

Gen 24:63-65

DAY 148

"The word of God is a bond. Hold unto it. He will fulfil His part".

19 God is not human, that he should lie, not a human being, that he should change his mind. Does he speak and then not act? Does he promise and not fulfill?

Numbers 23:19

21 Now the Lord was gracious to Sarah as he had said, and the Lord did for Sarah what he had promised. 2 Sarah became pregnant and bore a son to Abraham in his old age, at the very time God had promised him.

Gen 21:1-2

DAY 149

"Every gain outside Christ, is pain in the end"

30 "Woe to the obstinate children,"
declares the Lord, "to those who carry out plans that are not mine,   forming an alliance, but not by my Spirit,   heaping sin upon sin; 2 who go down to Egypt without consulting me;
who look for help to Pharaoh's protection,
to Egypt's shade for refuge.
3 But Pharaoh's protection will be to your shame,   Egypt's shade will bring you disgrace

Isaiah 30:1-3

DAY 150

"When God is excluded in any pursuit for help, it ends with pain. Involve Him all the way".

30 "Woe to the obstinate children," declares the Lord, "to those who carry out plans that are not mine, forming an alliance, but not by my Spirit, heaping sin upon sin; 2 who go down to Egypt without consulting me;
who look for help to Pharaoh's protection, to Egypt's shade for refuge.
3 But Pharaoh's protection will be to your shame, Egypt's shade will bring you disgrace

Isaiah 30:1-3

DAY 151

"God can keep a man from doing evil. Open up to him".

6 Then God said to him in the dream, "Yes, I know you did this with a clear conscience, and so I have kept you from sinning against me. That is why I did not let you touch her.

Gen 20:6

DAY 152

"Those who seek to take undue advantage of you, will greatly disadvantage themselves in the end. Just stay with God".

17 Then Abraham prayed to God, and God healed Abimelek, his wife and his female slaves so they could have children again, 18 for the Lord had kept all the women in Abimelek's household from conceiving because of Abraham's wife Sarah.

Gen 20:17-18

DAY 153

"If it regards his word, and keeping to his word, he will do everything for his word. Hold on to the word".

11 The matter distressed Abraham greatly because it concerned his son. 12 But God said to him, "Do not be so distressed about the boy and your slave woman. Listen to whatever Sarah tells you, because it is through Isaac that your offspring[a] will be reckoned. 13 I will make the son of the slave into a nation also, because he is your offspring."

Gen 21:11-13.

DAY 154

"Obedience is a key to supernatural provision and supply. Key into the business of obedience- it makes all the difference".

2 Then God said, "Take your son, your only son, whom you love—Isaac—and go to the region of Moriah. Sacrifice him there as a burnt offering on a mountain I will show you." 3 Early the next morning Abraham got up and loaded his donkey. He took with him two of his servants and his son Isaac. When he had cut enough wood for the burnt offering, he set out for the place God had told him about.

8 Abraham answered, "God himself will provide the lamb for the burnt offering, my son." And the two of them went on together.

11 But the angel of the Lord called out to him from

*heaven, "Abraham! Abraham!" "Here I am," he replied.
12 "Do not lay a hand on the boy," he said. "Do not do anything to him. Now I know that you fear God, because you have not withheld from me your son, your only son."
13 Abraham looked up and there in a thicket he saw a ram[a] caught by its horns. He went over and took the ram and sacrificed it as a burnt offering instead of his son.
14 So Abraham called that place The Lord Will Provide. And to this day it is said, "On the mountain of the Lord it will be provided."*

Gen 22:2-3, 8, 11-14

DAY 155

"Until you stay away, from what will keep you away from him, you will be far away from Him".

7 Submit yourselves, then, to God. Resist the devil, and he will flee from you. 8 Come near to God and he will come near to you. Wash your hands, you sinners, and purify your hearts, you double-minded.

James 4:7-8

DAY 156

"From lame to fame is what He does very well. Hold on and don't dare give up, the situation will turn around for your good- soon".

3 The king asked, "Is there no one still alive from the house of Saul to whom I can show God's kindness?" Ziba answered the king, "There is still a son of Jonathan; he is lame in both feet."

12 Mephibosheth had a young son named Mika, and all the members of Ziba's household were servants of Mephibosheth. 13 And Mephibosheth lived in Jerusalem, because he always ate at the king's table; he was lame in both feet

2 Samuel 9:3, 12-13

DAY 157

"Unless God delivers, when the devil targets you, what you try to do right, ends wrong sometimes".

15 I do not understand what I do. For what I want to do I do not do, but what I hate I do. 16 And if I do what I do not want to do, I agree that the law is good. 17 As it is, it is no longer I myself who do it, but it is sin living in me. 18 For I know that good itself does not dwell in me, that is, in my sinful nature.[a] For I have the desire to do what is good, but I cannot carry it out. 19 For I do not do the good I want to do, but the evil I do not want to do—this I keep on doing. 20 Now if I do what I do not want to do, it is no longer I who do it, but it is sin living in me that does it. 21 So I find this law at work: Although I want to do good, evil is right there with me. 22 For in my inner being I delight in God's law; 23 but I see another law at work in me, waging war against the law of my mind and making me a prisoner of the law of sin at work within me.

24 What a wretched man I am! Who will rescue me from this body that is subject to death? 25 Thanks be to God, who delivers me through Jesus Christ our Lord! So then, I myself in my mind am a slave to God's law, but in my sinful nature[b] a slave to the law of sin.

Romans 7:15-25

DAY 158

"When you seek Him, you will be sought after. Don't miss out".

12 They will be called the Holy People, the Redeemed of the Lord; and you will be called Sought After, the City No Longer Deserted.

Isaiah 62:12

DAY 159

Use what you know, to handle or solve what you don't know.

7 The fear of the Lord is the beginning of knowledge, but fools despise wisdom and instruction.

Proverbs 1:7

DAY 160

"You will never experience the greatness of God, leaving him standing at the door. Just let him in first."

²⁰ Here I am! I stand at the door and knock. If anyone hears my voice and opens the door, I will come in and eat with that person, and they with me.

Revelation 3:20

DAY 161

"The only thing that limits you, is everything outside the word. Stay with the word to be limitless in all you do, all you are, and all you would ever be".

[96] To all perfection I see a limit, but your commands are boundless.

Psalm 119:96

DAY 162

"The statutes of God give you a status beyond your teachers. Go for it"

*⁹⁹ I have more insight than all my teachers,
for I meditate on your statutes.*

Psalm 119:99

DAY 163

"God took your infirmities away- don't claim the devil's"

4 Surely he took up our pain and bore our suffering, yet we considered him punished by God, stricken by him, and afflicted. 5 But he was pierced for our transgressions, he was crushed for our iniquities;
the punishment that brought us peace was on him, and by his wounds we are healed. 6 We all, like sheep, have gone astray, each of us has turned to our own way; and the Lord has laid on him the iniquity of us all. 7 He was oppressed and afflicted, yet he did not open his mouth; he was led like a lamb to the slaughter, and as a sheep before its shearers is silent, so he did not open his mouth. 8 By oppression[a] and judgment he was taken away. Yet who of his generation protested?
For he was cut off from the land of the living; for the transgression of my people he was punished. 9 He was assigned a grave with the wicked, and with the rich in his death, though he had done no violence,

*nor was any deceit in his mouth. 10 Yet it was the Lord's will to crush him and cause him to suffer, and though the Lord makes[c] his life an offering for sin, he will see his offspring and prolong his days,
and the will of the Lord will prosper in his hand.*

Isaiah 53:4-10

DAY 164

"If you step out in the power of the word, you can stand on the word".

1 In the beginning was the Word, and the Word was with God, and the Word was God. 2 He was with God in the beginning. 3 Through him all things were made; without him nothing was made that has been made. 4 In him was life, and that life was the light of all mankind. 5 The light shines in the darkness, and the darkness has not overcome[a] it... 14 The Word became flesh and made his dwelling among us. We have seen his glory, the glory of the one and only Son, who came from the Father, full of grace and truth.

John 1:1-5, 14

DAY 165

"You have been empowered with understanding of the mysteries of the kingdom. Therefore, refuse confusion for direction".

11 He replied, "Because the knowledge of the secrets of the kingdom of heaven has been given to you, but not to them.

Mathew 13:11

DAY 166

"Until you are deeply rooted in what you claim and profess- you will not stand the test of time. Grow some roots".

*20 The seed falling on rocky ground refers to someone who hears the word and at once receives it with joy.
21 But since they have no root, they last only a short time. When trouble or persecution comes because of the word, they quickly fall away.*

Mathew 13:20-21

DAY 167

"If it's bad, then it couldn't have been God".

28 "'An enemy did this,' he replied. "The servants asked him, 'Do you want us to go and pull them up?'

Matthew 13:28

11 For I know the plans I have for you," declares the Lord, "plans to prosper you and not to harm you, plans to give you hope and a future.

Jeremiah 29:11

DAY 168

"When it loses value in your eyes, it loses its value also in your life".

55 "Isn't this the carpenter's son? Isn't his mother's name Mary, and aren't his brothers James, Joseph, Simon and Judas? 56 Aren't all his sisters with us? Where then did this man get all these things?" 57 And they took offense at him.

But Jesus said to them, "A prophet is not without honor except in his own town and in his own home."

58 And he did not do many miracles there because of their lack of faith.

Matthew 13:55-58

DAY 169

"Never allow familiarity with a vessel of blessing to cost you your blessings".

55 "Isn't this the carpenter's son? Isn't his mother's name Mary, and aren't his brothers James, Joseph, Simon and Judas? 56 Aren't all his sisters with us? Where then did this man get all these things?" 57 And they took offense at him.

But Jesus said to them, "A prophet is not without honour except in his own town and in his own home."

58 And he did not do many miracles there because of their lack of faith.

(Mathew 13:55-58).

DAY 170

"Too much focus on the problem and not the problem solver, could be the main problem. Look up and not around".

29 "Come," he said.

Then Peter got down out of the boat, walked on the water and came toward Jesus. 30 But when he saw the wind, he was afraid and, beginning to sink, cried out, "Lord, save me!"

Mathew14:29-30

DAY 171

"The truth is in the word. Go for the word".

31 To the Jews who had believed him, Jesus said, "If you hold to my teaching, you are really my disciples. 32 Then you will know the truth, and the truth will set you free."

John 8:31-32

DAY 172

"There is more life in front of you, than there is behind you. Quit dwelling on the past".

18 "Forget the former things; do not dwell on the past. 19 See, I am doing a new thing! Now it springs up; do you not perceive it? I am making a way in the wilderness and streams in the wasteland.

Isaiah 43:18-19

DAY 173

"If your desire is always for what you can't give, even when you have it, you could lose it easily. Be kind to all".

21 Then Peter came to Jesus and asked, "Lord, how many times shall I forgive my brother or sister who sins against me? Up to seven times?" 22 Jesus answered, "I tell you, not seven times, but seventy-seven times. 23 "Therefore, the kingdom of heaven is like a king who wanted to settle accounts with his servants. 24 As he began the settlement, a man who owed him ten thousand bags of gold was brought to him. 25 Since he was not able to pay, the master ordered that he and his wife and his children and all that he had be sold to repay the debt. 26 "At this the servant fell on his knees before him. 'Be patient with me,' he begged, 'and I will pay back everything.' 27 The servant's master took pity on him, canceled the debt and let him go. 28 "But when that servant went out, he found one of his fellow servants who owed him a hundred silver coins.[c] He grabbed him and began to choke him. 'Pay back what you owe me!' he demanded. 29 "His fellow servant fell to his knees and begged him, 'Be patient with me, and I will pay it back.'

30 "But he refused. Instead, he went off and had the man thrown into prison until he could pay the debt. 31 When the other servants saw what had happened, they were outraged and went and told their master everything that had happened. 32 "Then the master called the servant in. 'You wicked servant,' he said, 'I canceled all that debt of yours because you begged me to. 33 Shouldn't you have had mercy on your fellow servant just as I had on you?' 34 In anger his master handed him over to the jailers to be tortured, until he should pay back all he owed. 35 "This is how my heavenly Father will treat each of you unless you forgive your brother or sister from your heart."

Matthew 18:21-35

DAY 174

"Life's meaning is in its purpose. Discover the purpose".

21 Many are the plans in a person's heart, but it is the Lord's purpose that prevails.

Proverbs 19:21

DAY 175

"When the work of your hands is not blessed by God, it will not yield as much. Get him involved".

20 You may ask, "What will we eat in the seventh year if we do not plant or harvest our crops?" 21 I will send you such a blessing in the sixth year that the land will yield enough for three years. 22 While you plant during the eighth year, you will eat from the old crop and will continue to eat from it until the harvest of the ninth year comes in.

Leviticus 25:20-22

DAY 176

"Your fruit and harvest is not the by-product of your ability, but God's blessings. Make no mistake"

20 You may ask, "What will we eat in the seventh year if we do not plant or harvest our crops?" 21 I will send you such a blessing in the sixth year that the land will yield enough for three years. 22 While you plant during the eighth year, you will eat from the old crop and will continue to eat from it until the harvest of the ninth year comes in.

Leviticus 25:20-22

DAY 177

"You will easily miss the plot, the moment you begin to associate people's ability with their affinity or where they are coming from. Look beyond the origin".

53 When Jesus had finished these parables, he moved on from there. 54 Coming to his hometown, he began teaching the people in their synagogue, and they were amazed. "Where did this man get this wisdom and these miraculous powers?" they asked. 55 "Isn't this the carpenter's son? Isn't his mother's name Mary, and aren't his brothers James, Joseph, Simon and Judas? 56 Aren't all his sisters with us? Where then did this man get all these things?" 57 And they took offense at him.

But Jesus said to them, "A prophet is not without honor except in his own town and in his own home." 58 And he did not do many miracles there because of their lack of faith.

Mathew 13:53-58

DAY 178

"When He gives you an uncommon word or instruction, you don't need the common sense of men to carry it out".

15 But when God, who set me apart from my mother's womb and called me by his grace, was pleased 16 to reveal his Son in me so that I might preach him among the Gentiles, my immediate response was not to consult any human being. 17 I did not go up to Jerusalem to see those who were apostles before I was, but I went into Arabia. Later I returned to Damascus.

Gal 1:15-17

DAY 179

"Even when you are living apart from him, despite being set apart by him; He will bring you on the path in time".

15 But when God, who set me apart from my mother's womb and called me by his grace, was pleased 16 to reveal his Son in me so that I might preach him among the Gentiles, my immediate response was not to consult any human being. 17 I did not go up to Jerusalem to see those who were apostles before I was, but I went into Arabia. Later I returned to Damascus.

Gal 1:15-17

DAY 180

"The presence of God in your present situation, makes all the difference".

9 *"Because the patriarchs were jealous of Joseph, they sold him as a slave into Egypt. But God was with him.*

Acts 7:9

DAY 181

"The assurance of his presence in your present situation, secures your future".

9 "Because the patriarchs were jealous of Joseph, they sold him as a slave into Egypt. But God was with him 10 and rescued him from all his troubles. He gave Joseph wisdom and enabled him to gain the goodwill of Pharaoh king of Egypt. So Pharaoh made him ruler over Egypt and all his palace.

Acts 7:9-10

DAY 182

"You cannot present Him to your world beyond the level of the revelation you have of Him. Let Him reveal Himself more to you".

15 But when God, who set me apart from my mother's womb and called me by his grace, was pleased 16 to reveal his Son in me so that I might preach him among the Gentiles, my immediate response was not to consult any human being. 17 I did not go up to Jerusalem to see those who were apostles before I was, but I went into Arabia. Later I returned to Damascus.

Gal 1:15-17

DAY 183

"When God reveals himself to a man, he needs no approval of men".

15 But when God, who set me apart from my mother's womb and called me by his grace, was pleased 16 to reveal his Son in me so that I might preach him among the Gentiles, my immediate response was not to consult any human being. 17 I did not go up to Jerusalem to see those who were apostles before I was, but I went into Arabia. Later I returned to Damascus.

Gal 1:15-17

DAY 184

"You cannot run it your own way and win. Only his will and his way will prevail in the end".

21 Many are the plans in a person's heart, but it is the Lord's purpose that prevails.

Proverb 19:21

DAY 185

"When He goes before you, you have everything before you".

*This is what the Lord says to his anointed,
to Cyrus, whose right hand I take hold of
to subdue nations before him
and to strip kings of their armor,
to open doors before him
so that gates will not be shut:
2 I will go before you
and will level the mountains[a];
I will break down gates of bronze
and cut through bars of iron.*

Isaiah 45:1-2

DAY 186

"What so ever you are unwilling to pay a price for, has got little or no value to you"

2 fixing our eyes on Jesus, the pioneer and perfecter of faith. For the joy set before him he endured the cross, scorning its shame, and sat down at the right hand of the throne of God. 3 Consider him who endured such opposition from sinners, so that you will not grow weary and lose heart.

Hebrew 12: 2-3

DAY 187

"Very often, we have more than enough, to get us through what we complain about. Quit complaining"

10 Moses heard the people of every family wailing at the entrance to their tents. The Lord became exceedingly angry, and Moses was troubled. 11 He asked the Lord, "Why have you brought this trouble on your servant? What have I done to displease you that you put the burden of all these people on me? 12 Did I conceive all these people? Did I give them birth? Why do you tell me to carry them in my arms, as a nurse carries an infant, to the land you promised on oath to their ancestors? 13 Where can I get meat for all these people? They keep wailing to me, 'Give us meat to eat!' 14 I cannot carry all these people by myself; the burden is too heavy for me. 15 If this is how you are going to treat me, please go ahead and kill me—if I have found favor in your eyes—and do not let me face my own ruin."

16 The Lord said to Moses: "Bring me seventy of Israel's elders who are known to you as leaders and officials among the people. Have them come to the tent of meeting, that they may stand there with you. 17 I will come down and speak with you there, and I will take some of the power of the Spirit that is on you and put it on them. They will share the burden of the people with you so that you will not have to carry it alone

. Numbers 11:10-16, 17

DAY 189

"When God employs for an assignment, he empowers for that assignment. Don't quit, you are not alone"

21 But Moses said, "Here I am among six hundred thousand men on foot, and you say, 'I will give them meat to eat for a whole month!' 22 Would they have enough if flocks and herds were slaughtered for them? Would they have enough if all the fish in the sea were caught for them?" 23 The Lord answered Moses, "Is the Lord's arm too short? Now you will see whether or not what I say will come true for you."

24 So Moses went out and told the people what the Lord had said. He brought together seventy of their elders and had them stand around the tent. 25 Then the Lord came down in the cloud and spoke with him, and he took some of the power of the Spirit that was on him and put it on the seventy elders. When the Spirit rested on them, they prophesied—but did not do so again.

Numbers 11:21-25

DAY 190

"Until you see it differently, what you see obviously could deter you. See it God's way".

27 They gave Moses this account: "We went into the land to which you sent us, and it does flow with milk and honey! Here is its fruit. 28 But the people who live there are powerful, and the cities are fortified and very large. We even saw descendants of Anak there. 29 The Amalekites live in the Negev; the Hittites, Jebusites and Amorites live in the hill country; and the Canaanites live near the sea and along the Jordan."

30 Then Caleb silenced the people before Moses and said, "We should go up and take possession of the land, for we can certainly do it."

Numbers 13:27-30

DAY 191

"The greatness in us and the great things about us, are often seen in the little things we do. Do something, no matter how little".

38 When did we see you a stranger and invite you in, or needing clothes and clothe you? 39 When did we see you sick or in prison and go to visit you?' 40 "The King will reply, 'truly I tell you, whatever you did for one of the least of these brothers and sisters of mine, you did for me.'

Matthew 25:38-40

DAY 192

"Put on Jesus, not what the world is putting-on in their journey of life, it limits".

37 The Lord who rescued me from the paw of the lion and the paw of the bear will rescue me from the hand of this Philistine." Saul said to David, "Go, and the Lord be with you." 38 Then Saul dressed David in his own tunic. He put a coat of armor on him and a bronze helmet on his head. 39 David fastened on his sword over the tunic and tried walking around, because he was not used to them.

"I cannot go in these," he said to Saul, "because I am not used to them." So he took them off. 40 Then he took his staff in his hand, chose five smooth stones from the stream, put them in the pouch of his shepherd's bag and, with his sling in his hand, approached the Philistine.

1Samuel 17:37-40

DAY 193

"Watch how he treats those he does not need in his life, as it reflects the tendency, of how he would sometimes treat those he needs most".

9 Love must be sincere. Hate what is evil; cling to what is good. 10 Be devoted to one another in love. Honour one another above yourselves. 11 Never be lacking in zeal, but keep your spiritual fervor, serving the Lord. 12 Be joyful in hope, patient in affliction, faithful in prayer. 13 Share with the Lord's people who are in need. Practice hospitality.

14 Bless those who persecute you; bless and do not curse.

Romans 12:9-14

DAY 194

"What you do before a major decision, often determines the quality of the outcome. Jesus prayed, do likewise".

12 One of those days Jesus went out to a mountainside to pray, and spent the night praying to God. 13 When morning came, he called his disciples to him and chose twelve of them, whom he also designated apostles:

Luke 6:12-13

DAY 195

"The help you render, often would attract the help you need. Be helpful, you may need one someday".

4 When they came to Jesus, they pleaded earnestly with him, "This man deserves to have you do this, 5 because he loves our nation and has built our synagogue."

Luke 7:4-5

DAY 196

"The key to accessing the unknown will of God for your life, is obedience to the known will of God".

17 If anyone, then, knows the good they ought to do and doesn't do it, it is sin for them.

James 4:17

DAY 197

"If you think you are always right, then you are already wrong. Listen more and be teachable".

*20 Listen to advice and accept discipline,
and at the end you will be counted among the wise.*

Proverbs 19:20

DAY 198

"Let it be all about God, before it gets to you"

1 Shout for joy to the Lord, all the earth.
2 Worship the Lord with gladness;
come before him with joyful songs.
3 Know that the Lord is God.
It is he who made us, and we are his[a];
we are his people, the sheep of his pasture.

4 Enter his gates with thanksgiving
and his courts with praise;
give thanks to him and praise his name.
5 For the Lord is good and his love endures forever;
his faithfulness continues through all generations.

Psalm 100:1-5

DAY 199

"Every double visions is a di-vision which leads to confusion unless there is fusion of the two".

18 Where there is no vision, the people perish: but he that keepeth the law, happy is he.

Proverbs 29:18

21 Many are the plans in a person's heart,   but it is the Lord's purpose that prevails.

Proverbs 19:21

DAY 200

"Never settle where you are only supposed to pass through. There is much more to you and for you ahead, than where you are".

1 Terah took his son Abram, his grandson Lot son of Haran, and his daughter-in-law Sarai, the wife of his son Abram, and together they set out from Ur of the Chaldeans to go to Canaan. But when they came to Harran, they settled there. 32 Terah lived 205 years, and he died in Harran.

Genesis 11:31- 32

DAY 201

"Until you put a price on it, you could be priced-out of it".

44 "The kingdom of heaven is like treasure hidden in a field. When a man found it, he hid it again, and then in his joy went and sold all he had and bought that field.

45 "Again, the kingdom of heaven is like a merchant looking for fine pearls. 46 When he found one of great value, he went away and sold everything he had and bought it.

Mathew 13:44-46

DAY 202

"He acquaints you with good, when you acquaint yourself with him. Don't miss the good".

21 *"Submit to God and be at peace with him; in this way prosperity will come to you.*

Job 22:21

DAY 203

"Get it beyond your head to your heart, else, it will have no meaning to you".

22 Accept instruction from his mouth and lay up his words in your heart.

Job 22:22

DAY 204

"There is no returning to God, without a corresponding rebuilding and restoration by God".

*23 If you return to the Almighty, you will be restored:
If you remove wickedness far from your tent*

Job 22:23

DAY 205

"Even the common is not always common, but with God, he makes you very uncommon. Relate with him more for uncommon results".

10 so that you can distinguish between the holy and the common, between the unclean and the clean,

Leviticus 10:10

DAY 206

"Not only when you stop talking, do you lose intimacy with friends, but when you stop listening. Be teachable and cultivate a listening ear".

11 When Job's three friends, Eliphaz the Temanite, Bildad the Shuhite and Zophar the Naamathite, heard about all the troubles that had come upon him, they set out from their homes and met together by agreement to go and sympathize with him and comfort him. 12 When they saw him from a distance, they could hardly recognize him; they began to weep aloud, and they tore their robes and sprinkled dust on their heads. 13 Then they sat on the ground with him for seven days and seven nights. No one said a word to him, because they saw how great his suffering was.

Job 2:11-13

DAY 207

"If you don't pray in the boat, you will pray in the belly of ups and downs. Don't let it get there, pray".

The word of the Lord came to Jonah son of Amittai: 2 "Go to the great city of Nineveh and preach against it, because its wickedness has come up before me." 3 But Jonah ran away from the Lord and headed for Tarshish. He went down to Joppa, where he found a ship bound for that port. After paying the fare, he went aboard and sailed for Tarshish to flee from the Lord.

15 Then they took Jonah and threw him overboard, and the raging sea grew calm. 16 At this the men greatly feared the Lord, and they offered a sacrifice to the Lord and made vows to him. 17 Now the Lord provided a huge fish to swallow Jonah, and Jonah was in the belly of the fish three days and three nights.

Jonah 1:1-3, 15-17

DAY 208

"If you don't see God first, every man you set your eyes on, could confuse you and mess you up, because you saw him first".

Fixing our eyes on Jesus, the pioneer and perfecter of faith. For the joy set before him he endured the cross, scorning its shame, and sat down at the right hand of the throne of God.

Hebrew 12:2

DAY 209

"If Jesus were to be alive today, you possibly wouldn't date him, because he will not make it on your check-list. There was nothing desirable of him. Be careful with that your checklist".

Who has believed our message
and to whom has the arm of the Lord been revealed?
2 He grew up before him like a tender shoot,
and like a root out of dry ground.
He had no beauty or majesty to attract us to him,
nothing in his appearance that we should desire him.
3 He was despised and rejected by mankind,
a man of suffering, and familiar with pain.
Like one from whom people hide their faces
he was despised, and we held him in low esteem

Isaiah 53:1-3

DAY 210

"When a man fears God, his life revolves around God".

*16 No king is saved by the size of his army;
no warrior escapes by his great strength.
17 A horse is a vain hope for deliverance;
despite all its great strength it cannot save.
18 But the eyes of the Lord are on those who fear him,
on those whose hope is in his unfailing love,*

Psalm 33:16-18

DAY 211

"When the fear of God is absent in a man's life, the involvement of God in the man's affair becomes a story. Just fear God".

*16 No king is saved by the size of his army;
no warrior escapes by his great strength.
17 A horse is a vain hope for deliverance;
despite all its great strength it cannot save.
18 But the eyes of the Lord are on those who fear him,
on those whose hope is in his unfailing love,*

Psalm 33:16:18

DAY 212

"You don't need to have rooms around you, to make room for God"

7 and she gave birth to her firstborn, a son. She wrapped him in cloths and placed him in a manger, because there was no guest room available for them.

Luke 2:7

DAY 213

"She was not the only virgin in the land, but the favour of God located her anyway."

5 He went there to register with Mary, who was pledged to be married to him and was expecting a child. 6 While they were there, the time came for the baby to be born, 7 and she gave birth to her firstborn, a son. She wrapped him in cloths and placed him in a manger, because there was no guest room available for them.

Luke 2:5-7

DAY 214

"When you distance yourself from God, he excuses himself from you. Don't do that to yourself, just stay with God".

*30 How could one man chase a thousand,
or two put ten thousand to flight,
unless their Rock had sold them,
unless the Lord had given them up?*

Deuteronomy 32:30

DAY 215

"What you give, is a direct proportion of what you have in you. You can't give what you don't have".

46 he said to them, "Take to heart all the words I have solemnly declared to you this day, so that you may command your children to obey carefully all the words of this law.

Deuteronomy 32:46

DAY 216

"Not just your age, but also your star-attracts the enemy".

2 and asked, "Where is the one who has been born king of the Jews? We saw his star when it rose and have come to worship him."

3 When King Herod heard this he was disturbed, and all Jerusalem with him.

Mathew 2:2-3

DAY 217

"Even the devil is interested in your words. Use it rightly for God's glory".

13 Later they sent some of the Pharisees and Herodians to Jesus to catch him in his words.

Mark 12:13

DAY 218

"A genuine sense of leadership, guarantees complete submission from anyone and in anything. Lead when/where you need to, and submit when/where necessary".

21 Submit to one another out of reverence for Christ.

22 Wives, submit yourselves to your own husbands as you do to the Lord. 23 For the husband is the head of the wife as Christ is the head of the church, his body, of which he is the Savior. 24 Now as the church submits to Christ, so also wives should submit to their husbands in everything.

25 Husbands, love your wives, just as Christ loved the church and gave himself up for her 26 to make her holy, cleansing[a] her by the washing with water through the word, 27 and to present her to himself as a radiant church, without stain or wrinkle or any other blemish, but holy and blameless. 28 In this same way, husbands ought to love their wives as their own bodies. He who loves his wife loves himself. Ephesians 5:21-28

DAY 219

"When you are too busy for God, you stand the chance of never being used by God. Avail yourself".

18 As Jesus was walking beside the Sea of Galilee, he saw two brothers, Simon called Peter and his brother Andrew. They were casting a net into the lake, for they were fishermen. 19 "Come, follow me," Jesus said, "and I will send you out to fish for people." 20 At once they left their nets and followed him.

21 Going on from there, he saw two other brothers, James son of Zebedee and his brother John. They were in a boat with their father Zebedee, preparing their nets. Jesus called them, 22 and immediately they left the boat and their father and followed him.

Mathew 4:18-22

60 Jesus said to him, "Let the dead bury their own dead, but you go and proclaim the kingdom of God." 61 Still another said, "I will follow you, Lord; but first let me go back and say goodbye to my family." 62 Jesus replied, "No one who puts a hand to the plow and looks back is fit for service in the kingdom of God."

Luke 9:60-62

DAY 220

"When abnormality becomes normal, you live an abnormal life without knowing".

21 For although they knew God, they neither glorified him as God nor gave thanks to him, but their thinking became futile and their foolish hearts were darkened. 22 Although they claimed to be wise, they became fools 23 and exchanged the glory of the immortal God for images made to look like a mortal human being and birds and animals and reptiles.

24 Therefore God gave them over in the sinful desires of their hearts to sexual impurity for the degrading of their bodies with one another. 25 They exchanged the truth about God for a lie, and worshiped and served created things rather than the Creator—who is forever praised. Amen.

26 Because of this, God gave them over to shameful lusts. Even their women exchanged natural sexual relations for unnatural ones.

Romans 1: 21-26

DAY 221

"When his voice is absent, an alternative voice will for sure always be present. Be careful with noise".

32 If I fought wild beasts in Ephesus with no more than human hopes, what have I gained? If the dead are not raised,

"Let us eat and drink, for tomorrow we die." 33 Do not be misled: "Bad Company corrupts good character."

1 Corinthians 15:32-33

DAY 222

"Noise sets the tone for confusion. Be careful with noise".

18 Whoever conceals hatred with lying lips and spreads slander is a fool. 19 Sin is not ended by multiplying words, but the prudent hold their tongues. 20 The tongue of the righteous is choice silver,
but the heart of the wicked is of little value. 21 The lips of the righteous nourish many, but fools die for lack of sense

Proverbs 10:18-24

DAY 223

"The thorn in your flesh serves a purpose. Go through it with your eyes fixed on Jesus".

7 or because of these surpassingly great revelations. Therefore, in order to keep me from becoming conceited, I was given a thorn in my flesh, a messenger of Satan, to torment me. 8 Three times I pleaded with the Lord to take it away from me. 9 But he said to me, "My grace is sufficient for you, for my power is made perfect in weakness." Therefore I will boast all the more gladly about my weaknesses, so that Christ's power may rest on me.

2 Corinthians 12:7-9

DAY 224

"Your weakness should not deter you from God, he leverages on that, to show forth his glory to the world".

7 or because of these surpassingly great revelations. Therefore, in order to keep me from becoming conceited, I was given a thorn in my flesh, a messenger of Satan, to torment me. 8 Three times I pleaded with the Lord to take it away from me. 9 But he said to me, "My grace is sufficient for you, for my power is made perfect in weakness." Therefore I will boast all the more gladly about my weaknesses, so that Christ's power may rest on me.

2 Corinthians 12:7-9

25 For the foolishness of God is wiser than human wisdom, and the weakness of God is stronger than human strength.

1Corinthiants 1:25

DAY 225

"Don't be too quick to ask for what you are unwilling to give to others. Be kind to all and at all times".

2 He called a little child to him, and placed the child among them. 3 And he said: "Truly I tell you, unless you change and become like little children, you will never enter the kingdom of heaven. 4 Therefore, whoever takes the lowly position of this child is the greatest in the kingdom of heaven. 5 And whoever welcomes one such child in my name welcomes me. 6 "If anyone causes one of these little ones—those who believe in me—to stumble, it would be better for them to have a large millstone hung around their neck and to be drowned in the depths of the sea. 7 Woe to the world because of the things that cause people to stumble! Such things must come, but woe to the person through whom they come! 8 If your hand or your foot causes you to stumble, cut it off and throw it away. It is better for you to enter life maimed or crippled than to have two hands or two feet and be thrown into eternal fire. 9 And if your eye causes you to stumble, gouge it out and throw it away. It is better for you to enter life with one eye than to have two eyes and be thrown into the fire of hell. 10 "See that you do not despise one of these little ones. For I tell you that their angels in heaven always see the face of my Father in heaven. [11 12 "What do you think? If a man owns a hundred sheep, and one of them wanders away, will he not leave the ninety-nine on the hills and go to look for the one that wandered off? 13 And if he finds it, truly I tell you, he is happier about that one sheep than about the ninety-nine that did not wander off. 14 In the same way your Father in heaven is not willing that any of these little ones should perish. 15 "If your brother or sister[b] sins,[c] go and point out their fault, just between the two of you. If they listen to you, you have won them over. 16 But if they will not listen, take one or two others along, so that 'every matter may be established by the testimony of two or three witnesses.'[d] 17 If they still refuse to listen, tell it to the church; and if they refuse to listen even to the church, treat them as you would a pagan or a tax collector. 18 "Truly I tell you, whatever you bind on earth will be[e] bound in heaven, and whatever you loose on earth will be[f] loosed in heaven. 19 "Again, truly I tell you that if two of you on earth agree about anything they ask for, it will be done for them by my Father in heaven. 20 For where two or three gather in my name, there am I with them." 21 Then Peter came to Jesus and asked, "Lord, how many times shall I forgive my brother or sister who sins against me? Up to seven times?" 22 Jesus answered, "I tell you, not seven times, but seventy-seven times.[g] 23 "Therefore, the kingdom of heaven is like a king who wanted to settle accounts with his servants. 24 As he began the settlement, a man who owed him ten thousand bags of gold[h] was brought to him. 25 Since he was not able to pay, the master ordered that he and his wife and his children and all that he had be sold to repay the debt.

26 "At this the servant fell on his knees before him. 'Be patient with me,' he begged, 'and I will pay back everything.' 27 The servant's master took pity on him, canceled the debt and let him go. 28 "But when that servant went out, he found one of his fellow servants who owed him a hundred silver coins.[i] He grabbed him and began to choke him. 'Pay back what you owe me!' he demanded. 29 "His fellow servant fell to his knees and begged him, 'Be patient with me, and I will pay it back.' 30 "But he refused. Instead, he went off and had the man thrown into prison until he could pay the debt. 31 When the other servants saw what had happened, they were outraged and went and told their master everything that had happened. 32 "Then the master called the servant in. 'You wicked servant,' he said, 'I canceled all that debt of yours because you begged me to. 33 Shouldn't you have had mercy on your fellow servant just as I had on you?' 34 In anger his master handed him over to the jailers to be tortured, until he should pay back all he owed. 35 "This is how my heavenly Father will treat each of you unless you forgive your brother or sister from your heart."

Mathew 18:2-35

DAY 226

"Just a caretaker you are. God owns it all. Give it to him"

1 In the beginning God created the heavens and the earth.

Gen 1:1

8 'The silver is mine and the gold is mine,' declares the Lord Almighty.

Hagai 2:8

DAY 227

"Exult God and he will establish your greatness. He owns it all".

*Yours, Lord, is the greatness and the power
and the glory and the majesty and the splendor,
for everything in heaven and earth is yours.
Yours, Lord, is the kingdom;
you are exalted as head over all.
12 Wealth and honor come from you;
you are the ruler of all things.
In your hands are strength and power
to exalt and give strength to all.*

1chronicles 29:11-12

DAY 228

"If no man queries you, what about God? Avail yourself for accountability".

4 My conscience is clear, but that does not make me innocent. It is the Lord who judges me. 5 Therefore judge nothing before the appointed time; wait until the Lord comes. He will bring to light what is hidden in darkness and will expose the motives of the heart. At that time each will receive their praise from God.

1 Corinthians 4 :4-5

DAY 229

"It's not beyond your ability; you have all it takes to do well in what you have to do".

15 To one he gave five bags of gold, to another two bags, and to another one bag,[a] each according to his ability. Then he went on his journey.

Mathew 25:15

DAY 230

"Faith in God attracts forgiveness from God. Have faith"

5 "In Bethlehem in Judea," they replied, "for this is what the prophet has written:

Mathew 2:5

DAY 231

"Disobedience throws on you every life's worry for you to handle yourself, it's hectic. Just stay obedient and let God worry with your worries".

15 However, if you do not obey the Lord your God and do not carefully follow all his commands and decrees I am giving you today, all these curses will come on you and overtake you:

16 You will be cursed in the city and cursed in the country.

17 Your basket and your kneading trough will be cursed.

Deuteronomy 28:15-17

DAY 232

"The number of people faced with your kind of challenge, does not matter to God- he will single you out".

27 And there were many in Israel with leprosy in the time of Elisha the prophet, yet not one of them was cleansed— only Naaman the Syrian."

Luke 4:27

DAY 233

"Your association with Jesus, increases the expectation of the world about you. Don't disappoint them".

17 A man in the crowd answered, "Teacher, I brought you my son, who is possessed by a spirit that has robbed him of speech. 18 Whenever it seizes him, it throws him to the ground. He foams at the mouth, gnashes his teeth and becomes rigid. I asked your disciples to drive out the spirit, but they could not."

19 "You unbelieving generation," Jesus replied, "how long shall I stay with you? How long shall I put up with you? Bring the boy to me.

Mark 9:17-19

DAY 234

"The path to going up is serving others, not being served by others. Lavish yourself on it- it pays more in the end".

43 Not so with you. Instead, whoever wants to become great among you must be your servant, 44 and whoever wants to be first must be slave of all. 45 For even the Son of Man did not come to be served, but to serve, and to give his life as a ransom for many."

Mark 10:43-45

DAY 235

"What you do on hearing a good news-determines what you get out of the good news. Don't be quiet, act on the good news".

46 Then they came to Jericho. As Jesus and his disciples, together with a large crowd, were leaving the city, a blind man, Bartimaeus (which means "son of Timaeus"), was sitting by the roadside begging. 47 When he heard that it was Jesus of Nazareth, he began to shout, "Jesus, Son of David, have mercy on me!" 48 Many rebuked him and told him to be quiet, but he shouted all the more, "Son of David, have mercy on me!" 49 Jesus stopped and said, "Call him." So they called to the blind man, "Cheer up! On your feet! He's calling you."

Mark 10:46-49

DAY 236

"God also deserves much more than the world is demanding from you. Don't do his work with attitude".

[10] *"A curse on anyone who is lax in doing the Lord's work!*
Jeremiah 48:10a

DAY 237

"You could end yourself in trouble, when you refuse others the access to rebuke you. Be accountable"

15 A rod and a reprimand impart wisdom, but a child left undisciplined disgraces its mother.

Proverbs 29:15

DAY 238

"Not all the troubles in our lives are brought on us, we get to some with our hands. Watch it".

10 Then Judas Iscariot, one of the Twelve, went to the chief priests to betray Jesus to them. 11 They were delighted to hear this and promised to give him money. So he watched for an opportunity to hand him over.

Mark 14:10-11

DAY 239

"When you look up to who is bigger than you, everything around you that seems bigger than you- submits to you. Just keep looking up".

2 Very early on the first day of the week, just after sunrise, they were on their way to the tomb 3 and they asked each other, "Who will roll the stone away from the entrance of the tomb?"

4 But when they looked up, they saw that the stone, which was very large, had been rolled away.

Mark 16:2-4

DAY 240

"If it's not from the Lord, sorrow may accompany it. Be careful".

22 The blessing of the Lord brings wealth, without painful toil for it.

Proverbs 10:22

DAY 241

"When you lose touch with your source, the enemy will not have to be more powerful than you to defeat you. Stay connected to your main source (God)"

25 The Lord will cause you to be defeated before your enemies. You will come at them from one direction but flee from them in seven, and you will become a thing of horror to all the kingdoms on earth.

Deuteronomy 28:25

DAY 242

"You don't have to be told, to be caring. Be observant and show some care. It goes a long way"

8 During those days another large crowd gathered. Since they had nothing to eat, Jesus called his disciples to him and said, 2 "I have compassion for these people; they have already been with me three days and have nothing to eat. 3 If I send them home hungry, they will collapse on the way, because some of them have come a long distance." 4 His disciples answered, "But where in this remote place can anyone get enough bread to feed them?" 5 "How many loaves do you have?" Jesus asked. "Seven," they replied. 6 He told the crowd to sit down on the ground. When he had taken the seven loaves and given thanks, he broke them and gave them to his disciples to distribute to the people, and they did so.

Mark 8:1-6

DAY 243

"A man's religion should be worn in his heart, not the lapel of his coat. Do what you say".

"Do not keep talking so proudly or let your mouth speak such arrogance, for the Lord is a God who knows, and by him deeds are weighed.

1 Samuel 2:3

DAY 244

"Until you allow him to play the main role in your life, you cannot attain the major things in life. Let him be the first in all"

2 Looking unto Jesus the author and finisher of our faith; who for the joy that was set before him endured the cross, despising the shame, and is set down at the right hand of the throne of God.

Hebrews 12:2

DAY 245

"Don't be too quick to give up, even if the people around you, supporting you, fighting with you- try to kill you. There is strength with God".

6 David was greatly distressed because the men were talking of stoning him; each one was bitter in spirit because of his sons and daughters. But David found strength in the Lord his God.

1 Samuel 30:6

DAY 246

"He (Devil) leverages on the ignorance of men, to damage the lives of men, don't be ignorant".

6 My people are destroyed for lack of knowledge: because thou hast rejected knowledge, I will also reject thee, that thou shalt be no priest to me: seeing thou hast forgotten the law of thy God, I will also forget thy children.

Hosea 4:6

5 The devil led him up to a high place and showed him in an instant all the kingdoms of the world. 6 And he said to him, "I will give you all their authority and splendor; it has been given to me, and I can give it to anyone I want to. 7 If you worship me, it will all be yours."

Luke 4:5-7

DAY 247

"Until you see what you are seeing, as having everything for you in it, you'll hardly leave everything for it. Let Christ be seen that way".

6 When they had done so, they caught such a large number of fish that their nets began to break. 7 So they signalled their partners in the other boat to come and help them, and they came and filled both boats so full that they began to sink.

8 When Simon Peter saw this, he fell at Jesus' knees and said, "Go away from me, Lord; I am a sinful man!" 9 For he and all his companions were astonished at the catch of fish they had taken, 10 and so were James and John, the sons of Zebedee, Simon's partners.

Then Jesus said to Simon, "Don't be afraid; from now on you will fish for people." 11 So they pulled their boats up on shore, left everything and followed him

Luke 5:6-11

DAY 248

"Your capacity to accommodate the people in your life, should not just be when they are at their best only, but also in their mess as well"

22 David left Gath and escaped to the cave of Adullam. When his brothers and his father's household heard about it, they went down to him there. 2 All those who were in distress or in debt or discontented gathered around him, and he became their commander. About four hundred men were with him.

1 Samuel 22:1-2

DAY 249

"You will always reproduce just what you are. Be a good one"

43 "No good tree bears bad fruit, nor does a bad tree bear good fruit. 44 Each tree is recognized by its own fruit. People do not pick figs from thorn bushes, or grapes from briers. 45 A good man brings good things out of the good stored up in his heart, and an evil man brings evil things out of the evil stored up in his heart. For the mouth speaks what the heart is full of.

Luke 6:43-45

DAY 250

"You live life either in credit or on credit. Don't feast on your tomorrow today".

*14 This is why it is said: "Wake up, sleeper, rise from the dead,
and Christ will shine on you." 15 Be very careful, then, how you live—not as unwise but as wise, 16 making the most of every opportunity, because the days are evil. 17 Therefore do not be foolish, but understand what the Lord's will is.*

Ephesians 5:14-17

DAY 251

"There is no wisdom in having wisdom, and not applying wisdom. Apply it- it pays more".

*Listen, my sons, to a father's instruction; pay attention and gain understanding.
2 I give you sound learning, so do not forsake my teaching. 3 For I too was a son to my father, still tender, and cherished by my mother. 4 Then he taught me, and he said to me, "Take hold of my words with all your heart; keep my commands, and you will live.
5 Get wisdom, get understanding; do not forget my words or turn away from them.
6 Do not forsake wisdom, and she will protect you; love her, and she will watch over you. 7 The beginning of wisdom is this: Get[a] wisdom. Though it cost all you have,[b] get understanding. 8 Cherish her, and she will exalt you; embrace her, and she will honour you.*

Proverbs 4:1-8

DAY 252

"The absence of a sound mind makes a shameful act seem shameless to the perpetrator. Stay in your right mind"

27 When Jesus stepped ashore, he was met by a demon-possessed man from the town. For a long time this man had not worn clothes or lived in a house, but had lived in the tombs. 28 When he saw Jesus, he cried out and fell at his feet, shouting at the top of his voice, "What do you want with me, Jesus, Son of the Most High God? I beg you, don't torture me!" 29 For Jesus had commanded the impure spirit to come out of the man. Many times it had seized him, and though he was chained hand and foot and kept under guard, he had broken his chains and had been driven by the demon into solitary places.

30 Jesus asked him, "What is your name?" "Legion," he replied, because many demons had gone into him. 31 And they begged Jesus repeatedly not to order them to go into the Abyss.

32 A large herd of pigs was feeding there on the hillside. The demons begged Jesus to let them go into the pigs, and he gave them permission. 33 When the demons came out of the man, they went into the pigs, and the herd rushed down the steep bank into the lake and was drowned. 34 When those tending the pigs saw what had happened, they ran off and reported this in the town and countryside, 35 and the people went out to see what had happened. When they came to Jesus, they found the man from whom the demons had gone out, sitting at Jesus' feet, dressed and in his right mind; and they were afraid.

Luke 8:27-35

DAY 253

"The deliverance of God, is often tied-down to an assignment from God. Don't rush out or run-away"

38 The man from whom the demons had gone out begged to go with him, but Jesus sent him away, saying, 39 "Return home and tell how much God has done for you." So the man went away and told all over town how much Jesus had done for him.

Luke 8: 38-39

DAY 254

"Never refuse or run away from help when it comes, it's in dear need somewhere, make the most of it".

37 Then all the people of the region of the Gerasenes asked Jesus to leave them, because they were overcome with fear. So he got into the boat and left.

*38 The man from whom the demons had gone out begged to go with him, but Jesus sent him away, saying,
39 "Return home and tell how much God has done for you." So the man went away and told all over town how much Jesus had done for him.*

40 Now when Jesus returned, a crowd welcomed him, for they were all expecting him.

Luke 8:37- 40

DAY 255

"He leaves a point of reference for every revelation. Refer to it always".

17 Jesus replied, "Blessed are you, Simon son of Jonah, for this was not revealed to you by flesh and blood, but by my Father in heaven. 18 And I tell you that you are Peter, and on this rock I will build my church, and the gates of Hades will not overcome it.

Matthew 16:17-18

DAY 256

"Whatever dares his authority, pulls him to act. Don't be afraid, just believe"

43 And a woman was there who had been subject to bleeding for twelve years,[a] but no one could heal her. 44 She came up behind him and touched the edge of his cloak, and immediately her bleeding stopped.

45 "Who touched me?" Jesus asked. When they all denied it, Peter said, "Master, the people are crowding and pressing against you." 46 But Jesus said, "Someone touched me; I know that power has gone out from me."

47 Then the woman, seeing that she could not go unnoticed, came trembling and fell at his feet. In the presence of all the people, she told why she had touched him and how she had been instantly healed. 48 Then he said to her, "Daughter, your faith has healed you. Go in peace."49 While Jesus was still speaking, someone came from the house of Jairus, the synagogue leader. "Your daughter is dead," he said. "Don't bother the teacher anymore." 50 Hearing this, Jesus said to Jairus, "Don't be afraid; just believe, and she will be healed."

Luke 8:43-50

DAY 257

"You are a spirit not just a body. Invest more on it, it pays more".

52 Meanwhile, all the people were wailing and mourning for her. "Stop wailing," Jesus said. "She is not dead but asleep."

53 They laughed at him, knowing that she was dead. 54 But he took her by the hand and said, "My child, get up!" 55 Her spirit returned, and at once she stood up. Then Jesus told them to give her something to eat. 56 Her parents were astonished, but he ordered them not to tell anyone what had happened.

Luke 8:52-56

DAY 258

"The main mistake is not always the mistake itself, but the fear that you will make one, is the greatest mistake. Dare something fearlessly"

13 I can do all things through Christ[a] who strengthens me.

Philippians 4:13

DAY 259

"Whatever you distance yourself from, distances itself from you. Stay close to what adds value to your life".

7 Therefore submit to God. Resist the devil and he will flee from you.

James 4:7

DAY 260

"You will always see what others can't see, when you see God. Fix your eyes on him".

23 Then he turned to his disciples and said privately, "Blessed are the eyes that see what you see. 24 For I tell you that many prophets and kings wanted to see what you see but did not see it, and to hear what you hear but did not hear it."

Luke 10:23-24

DAY 261

"You frustrate your learning, when you worry more on the minors at the expense of the majors"

41 "Martha, Martha," the Lord answered, "you are worried and upset about many things, 42 but few things are needed—or indeed only one.[a] Mary has chosen what is better, and it will not be taken away from her."

Luke 10:41-42

DAY 262

"You will get what you want, if you refuse to get away from what you want. Stay audacious in your pursuits".

8 I tell you, even though he will not get up and give you the bread because of friendship, yet because of your shameless audacity[a] he will surely get up and give you as much as you need.

9 "So I say to you: Ask and it will be given to you; seek and you will find; knock and the door will be opened to you. 10 For everyone who asks receives; the one who seeks finds; and to the one who knocks, the door will be opened.

Luke 11:8-10

DAY 263

"When you take a stand, the world stands in wait also for your contradiction. Don't have double standard".

53 When Jesus went outside, the Pharisees and the teachers of the law began to oppose him fiercely and to besiege him with questions, 54 waiting to catch him in something he might say.

Luke 11:53-54

DAY 264

"The meaninglessness of life will catch up with you, when your pursuits in life are only on the meaningless things of life. Pursue purpose".

If in this life only we have hope in Christ, we are of all men most miserable

1 Cornthians 15:19

DAY 265

"I will not be tricked into releasing the best of me, in the worst of places. Watch out". (Prayer)

21 Isaac said to Jacob, "Please come near, that I may feel you, my son, whether you are really my son Esau or not." 22 So Jacob went near to Isaac his father, and he felt him and said, "The voice is Jacob's voice, but the hands are the hands of Esau." 23 And he did not recognize him, because his hands were hairy like his brother Esau's hands; so he blessed him.

24 Then he said, "Are you really my son Esau?" He said, "I am."

25 He said, "Bring it near to me, and I will eat of my son's game, so that my soul may bless you." So he brought it near to him, and he ate; and he brought him wine, and he drank. 26 Then his father Isaac said to him, "Come near now and kiss me, my son." 27 And he came near and kissed him; and he smelled the smell of his clothing, and blessed him and said:

"Surely, the smell of my son is like the smell of a field which the Lord has blessed. 28 Therefore may God give you of the dew of heaven, of the fatness of the earth, And plenty of grain and wine. 29 Let peoples serve you, and nations bow down to you. Be master over your brethren, And let your other's sons bow down to you. Cursed be everyone who curses you, And blessed be those who bless you!"

33 Then Isaac trembled exceedingly, and said, "Who? Where is the one who hunted game and brought it to me? I ate all of it before you came, and I have blessed him— and indeed he shall be blessed."

Gen 27:21-29, 33

DAY 266

"Don't let it away the first time; losing it the second time will be normal".

54 Then seizing him, they led him away and took him into the house of the high priest. Peter followed at a distance. 55 And when some there had kindled a fire in the middle of the courtyard and had sat down together, Peter sat down with them. 56 A servant girl saw him seated there in the firelight. She looked closely at him and said, "This man was with him." 57 But he denied it. "Woman, I don't know him," he said. 58 A little later someone else saw him and said, "You also are one of them." "Man, I am not!" Peter replied. 59 About an hour later another asserted, "Certainly this fellow was with him, for he is a Galilean."

60 Peter replied, "Man, I don't know what you're talking about!" Just as he was speaking, the rooster crowed. 61 The Lord turned and looked straight at Peter. Then

Peter remembered the word the Lord had spoken to him: "Before the rooster crows today, you will disown me three times." 62 And he went outside and wept bitterly.

Luke 22:54-62

DAY 267

"Your place in life is the function of your purpose for life. Live purposefully"

34 *"Salt is good, but if it loses its saltiness, how can it be made salty again? 35 It is fit neither for the soil nor for the manure pile; it is thrown out.*

"Whoever has ears to hear, let them hear"

Luke 14:34-35

DAY 268

"You cannot go through life, with Jesus as your reference for life, without your name being referenced in life."

43 And a woman was there who had been subject to bleeding for twelve years,[a] but no one could heal her. 44 She came up behind him and touched the edge of his cloak, and immediately her bleeding stopped.

45 "Who touched me?" Jesus asked. When they all denied it, Peter said, "Master, the people are crowding and pressing against you." 46 But Jesus said, "Someone touched me; I know that power has gone out from me."

47 Then the woman, seeing that she could not go unnoticed, came trembling and fell at his feet. In the presence of all the people, she told why she had touched him and how she had been instantly healed. 48 Then he said to her, "Daughter, your faith has healed you. Go in peace."

Luke 8:43-48

DAY 269

"You don't need anything or anyone around you that is not worth having you"

20 So the man gave names to all the livestock, the birds in the sky and all the wild animals. But for Adam[a] no suitable helper was found. 21 So the Lord God caused the man to fall into a deep sleep; and while he was sleeping, he took one of the man's ribs[b] and then closed up the place with flesh. 22 Then the Lord God made a woman from the rib[c] he had taken out of the man, and he brought her to the man. 23 The man said,

*"This is now bone of my bones and flesh of my flesh; she shall be called 'woman,'
for she was taken out of man."*

Gen 2:20-23

DAY 270

"When you refuse to be hired for the right cause, you can't escape being hired for the wrong one".

15 So he went and hired himself out to a citizen of that country, who sent him to his fields to feed pigs.

Luke 15:15

DAY 271

"It doesn't matter what you have helped life in doing with your life- there is no place like home. Just set back".

17 "When he came to his senses, he said, 'How many of my father's hired servants have food to spare, and here I am starving to death! 18 I will set out and go back to my father and say to him: Father, I have sinned against heaven and against you. 19 I am no longer worthy to be called your son; make me like one of your hired servants.'

Luke 15:17-19

DAY 272

"The church wants the world to come to church; and when the world comes to church, the church has a problem with the world. What should the world do?"

25 "Meanwhile, the older son was in the field. When he came near the house, he heard music and dancing. 26 So he called one of the servants and asked him what was going on. 27 'Your brother has come,' he replied, 'and your father has killed the fattened calf because he has him back safe and sound.'

28 "The older brother became angry and refused to go in. So his father went out and pleaded with him. 29 But he answered his father, 'Look! All these years I've been slaving for you and never disobeyed your orders. Yet you never gave me even a young goat so I could celebrate with my friends. 30 But when this son of yours who has squandered your property with prostitutes comes home, you kill the fattened calf for him!'

Luke 15:25-30

DAY 273

"The church has a problem with the world, because the church does not know what she owns".

31 "'my son,' the father said, 'you are always with me, and everything I have is yours.

Luke 15:31

DAY 274

"If he can get you out of your mind, he will get you away from your inheritance. Refuse to lose your mind".

17 "When he came to his senses, he said, 'How many of my father's hired servants have food to spare, and here I am starving to death! 18 I will set out and go back to my father and say to him: Father, I have sinned against heaven and against you. 19 I am no longer worthy to be called your son; make me like one of your hired servants.'

Luke 15:17-19

DAY 275

"Fruits take a long time to come out. Don't abort the process"

21 The Lord smelled the pleasing aroma and said in his heart: "Never again will I curse the ground because of humans, even though[a] every inclination of the human heart is evil from childhood. And never again will I destroy all living creatures, as I have done. 22 "As long as the earth endures, seedtime and harvest, cold and heat, summer and winter, day and night will never cease

Genesis 8:21-22

DAY 276

"The best things of life, often cannot be accessed by strength-but God's favour"

4 Remain in me, as I also remain in you. No branch can bear fruit by itself; it must remain in the vine. Neither can you bear fruit unless you remain in me.

John 15:4

DAY 277

"The greatest influence, is often the unseen one. Quit the obvious".

33 He told them still another parable: "The kingdom of heaven is like yeast that a woman took and mixed into about sixty pounds[a] of flour until it worked all through the dough."

Matthew 13:33

DAY 278

"The evidence of fruitfulness, is the fruits. Produce some as evidence".

9 And do not think you can say to yourselves, 'We have Abraham as our father.' I tell you that out of these stones God can raise up children for Abraham. 10 The ax is already at the root of the trees, and every tree that does not produce good fruit will be cut down and thrown into the fire.

Mathew 3:9-10

DAY 279

"You can only have access to what you are ready for. Mature, to access and benefit more"

3 Brothers and sisters, I could not address you as people who live by the Spirit but as people who are still worldly— mere infants in Christ.

1 Corinthians 3:1

DAY 280

"What a tragedy, to walk like a man who is in his right mind- but yet, out of his mind. May his mind be in you".

5 In your relationships with one another, have the same mind-set as Christ Jesus:

Philipians 2:5

DAY 281

"What you should do, but refused to do in comfort, you may not escape doing it in pain".

27 "He answered, 'Then I beg you, father, send Lazarus to my family, 28 for I have five brothers. Let him warn them, so that they will not also come to this place of torment.'

29 "Abraham replied, 'They have Moses and the Prophets; let them listen to them.'

Luke 16:27-29

DAY 282

"When power changes hand, those who bullied you before, will not have access to you, to bully you again. Stay on the winning side"

24 "Then he cried and said, 'Father Abraham, have mercy on me, and send Lazarus that he may dip the tip of his finger in water and cool my tongue; for I am tormented in this flame.' 25 But Abraham said, 'Son, remember that in your lifetime you received your good things, and likewise Lazarus evil things; but now he is comforted and you are tormented. 26 And besides all this, between us and you there is a great gulf fixed, so that those who want to pass from here to you cannot, nor can those from there pass to us.'

27 "Then he said, 'I beg you therefore, father, that you would send him to my father's house, 28 for I have five brothers, that he may testify to them, lest they also come to this place of torment.' 29 Abraham said to him, 'They have Moses and the prophets; let them hear them.' 30 And he said, 'No, father Abraham; but if one goes to them from the dead, they will repent.'

Luke 16:24-30

DAY 283

"Fruitlessness in a place, does not necessarily mean fruitlessness in your life. Just stay fruitful in your relationship with God"

26 1 Now there was a famine in the land—besides the previous famine in Abraham's time—and Isaac went to Abimelek king of the Philistines in Gerar. 2 The Lord appeared to Isaac and said, "Do not go down to Egypt; live in the land where I tell you to live.

12 Then Isaac sowed in that land, and reaped in the same year a hundredfold; and the Lord blessed him.

Gen 26:1-2, 12

DAY 284

"It's tragic, to operate under a closed heaven. Let it stay open".

20 And your strength shall be spent in vain; for your land shall not yield its produce, nor shall the trees of the land yield their fruit

*6 "You have sown much, and bring in little;
You eat, but do not have enough;
You drink, but you are not filled with drink;
You clothe yourselves, but no one is warm;
And he who earns wages,
Earns wages to put into a bag with holes."*

Levi 26:20; Haggai 1:6

DAY 285

"He expects an attitude of gratitude. Don't be ungrateful".

11 Now on his way to Jerusalem, Jesus travelled along the border between Samaria and Galilee. 12 As he was going into a village, ten men who had leprosy[a] met him. They stood at a distance 13 and called out in a loud voice, "Jesus, Master, have pity on us!"

14 When he saw them, he said, "Go, show yourselves to the priests." And as they went, they were cleansed. 15 One of them, when he saw he was healed, came back, praising God in a loud voice. 16 He threw himself at Jesus' feet and thanked him—and he was a Samaritan.

17 Jesus asked, "Were not all ten cleansed? Where are the other nine? 18 Has no one returned to give praise to God except this foreigner?" 19 Then he said to him, "Rise and go; your faith has made you well."

Luke 17:11-19

DAY 286

"Your presence in a place, could propel, prevent or delay the occurrence of certain tragedies in that place".

27 People were eating, drinking, marrying and being given in marriage up to the day Noah entered the ark. Then the flood came and destroyed them all.

28 "It was the same in the days of Lot. People were eating and drinking, buying and selling, planting and building. 29 But the day Lot left Sodom, fire and sulfur rained down from heaven and destroyed them all.

Luke 17:27-29

DAY 287

"It's not the size of what you have in life that gives you what you want for life, but the size of who you have in life".

6 He replied, "If you have faith as small as a mustard seed, you can say to this mulberry tree, 'Be uprooted and planted in the sea,' and it will obey you.

Luke 17:6

DAY 288

"Until you approach him with a definite thing, you could leave without having a definite thing from him."

40 Jesus stopped and ordered the man to be brought to him. When he came near, Jesus asked him, 41 "What do you want me to do for you?"

"Lord, I want to see," he replied. 42 Jesus said to him, "Receive your sight; your faith has healed you."

Luke 18:40-42

DAY 289

"You are loaded for life, when he downloads His life in you. Insert your device".

15 For I will give you words and wisdom that none of your adversaries will be able to resist or contradict

Luke 21:15

DAY 290

"God doesn't need you, to be what he is, he is all by himself, what he is. Don't give or serve him with attitude."

37When he came near the place where the road goes down the Mount of Olives, the whole crowd of disciples began joyfully to praise God in loud voices for all the miracles they had seen:

38 "Blessed is the king who comes in the name of the Lord!"[a]

"Peace in heaven and glory in the highest!"

39 Some of the Pharisees in the crowd said to Jesus, "Teacher, rebuke your disciples!"

40 "I tell you," he replied, "if they keep quiet, the stones will cry out."

(Luke 19:37-40)

DAY 291

"When you allow the interruption of heaven in your life, it empowers you to be able to disrupt the flow of men's activities for good".

37 Each day Jesus was teaching at the temple, and each evening he went out to spend the night on the hill called the Mount of Olives, 38 and all the people came early in the morning to hear him at the temple.

Luke 21:37-38

DAY 292

"When you refuse to find Jesus, the devil will find in your life what he wants, and what he is looking for, for evil".

2 and the chief priests and the teachers of the law were looking for some way to get rid of Jesus, for they were afraid of the people. 3 Then Satan entered Judas, called Iscariot, one of the Twelve. 4 And Judas went to the chief priests and the officers of the temple guard and discussed with them how he might betray Jesus. 5 They were delighted and agreed to give him money.

Luke 22:2-5

DAY 293

"If he sends you, he will send help. Quit worrying".

35 Then Jesus asked them, "When I sent you without purse, bag or sandals, did you lack anything?" "Nothing," they answered.

Luke 22:35

DAY 294

"Wherever and whatever God has not given to you, there is no victory for you in it. Don't go it alone".

5 Do not provoke them to war, for I will not give you any of their land, not even enough to put your foot on. I have given Esau the hill country of Seir as his own.

9 Then the Lord said to me, "Do not harass the Moabites or provoke them to war, for I will not give you any part of their land. I have given Ar to the descendants of Lot as a possession."

Deut 2:5,9

DAY 295

"Progression is in the nature of God, don't stagnate or get yourself stuck in a place for too long. Break camp and advance".

6 The Lord our God said to us at Horeb, "You have stayed long enough at this mountain. 7 Break camp and advance into the hill country of the Amorites; go to all the neighboring peoples in the Arabah, in the mountains, in the western foothills, in the Negev and along the coast, to the land of the Canaanites and to Lebanon, as far as the great river, the Euphrates.

Deut 1:6-7; 2:2-3

DAY 296

"When you refuse his instructions, you give him reasons to regret making you what you are".

35 Until the day Samuel died, he did not go to see Saul again, though Samuel mourned for him. And the Lord regretted that he had made Saul king over Israel.

1 Samuel 15:35

DAY 297

"Anyone doing God's work, God's way, is important in God's eyes. Size doesn't count".

6 So he said to me, "This is the word of the Lord to Zerubbabel: 'Not by might nor by power, but by my Spirit,' says the Lord Almighty.

Zechariah 4:6

DAY 298

"Size and number only count in what you do for a living, not what you do to make a difference. Just do it big where you are".

6 So he said to me, "This is the word of the Lord to Zerubbabel: 'Not by might nor by power, but by my Spirit,' says the Lord Almighty.

Zechariah 4:6

DAY 299

"Never stay too long in a place, without making much progress. He frowns at it, unless he says so".

6 "The Lord our God spoke to us in Horeb, saying: 'You have dwelt long enough at this mountain. 7 Turn and take your journey, and go to the mountains of the Amorites, to all the neighboring places in the plain,[a] in the mountains and in the lowland, in the South and on the seacoast, to the land of the Canaanites and to Lebanon, as far as the great river, the River Euphrates.

Deut 1:6-7

DAY 300

"It takes only God's grace to overcome jealousy and bitterness, to encourage someone to take over a position which you have lost".

37 Because of you the Lord became angry with me also and said, "You shall not enter it, either. 38 But your assistant, Joshua son of Nun, will enter it. Encourage him, because he will lead Israel to inherit it.

Deut 1:37-38

DAY 301

"When you step out without him leading you, victory cannot be guaranteed; but defeat is almost certain. Involve him in it".

42 But the Lord said to me, "Tell them, 'Do not go up and fight, because I will not be with you. You will be defeated by your enemies.'" 43 So I told you, but you would not listen. You rebelled against the Lord's command and in your arrogance you marched up into the hill country. 44 The Amorites who lived in those hills came out against you; they chased you like a swarm of bees and beat you down from Seir all the way to Hormah. 45 You came back and wept before the Lord, but he paid no attention to your weeping and turned a deaf ear to you.

(Deut 1:42-45)

DAY 302

"When he commands you to move and you refuse, only to move in your own time, you will easily suffer casualty".

6 The Lord our God said to us at Horeb, "You have stayed long enough at this mountain. 7 Break camp and advance into the hill country of the Amorites; go to all the neighbouring peoples in the Arabah, in the mountains, in the western foothills, in the Negev and along the coast, to the land of the Canaanites and to Lebanon, as far as the great river, the Euphrates…….. 26 But you were unwilling to go up; you rebelled against the command of the Lord your God. 27 You grumbled in your tents and said, "The Lord hates us; so he brought us out of Egypt to deliver us into the hands of the Amorites to destroy us. 28 Where can we go? Our brothers have made our hearts melt in fear. They say, 'The people are stronger and taller than we are; the cities are large, with walls up to the sky. We even saw the Anakites there.'" ......42 But the Lord said to me, "Tell them, 'Do not go up and fight, because I will not be with you. You will be defeated by your enemies.'" 43 So I told you, but you would not listen. You rebelled against the Lord's command and in your arrogance you marched up into the hill country. 44 The Amorites who lived in those hills came out against you; they chased you like a swarm of bees and beat you down from Seir all the way to Hormah. 45 You came back and wept before the Lord, but he paid no attention to your weeping and turned a deaf ear to you. 46 And so you stayed in Kadesh many days— all the time you spent there.

(Deut 1:6-7;26-32;42-46)

DAY 303

"You will spend too much time where you are without progress, when you are not spontaneous to his instruction".

6 The Lord our God said to us at Horeb, "You have stayed long enough at this mountain. 7 Break camp and advance into the hill country of the Amorites; go to all the neighbouring peoples in the Arabah, in the mountains, in the western foothills, in the Negev and along the coast, to the land of the Canaanites and to Lebanon, as far as the great river, the Euphrates…….. 26 But you were unwilling to go up; you rebelled against the command of the Lord your God. 27 You grumbled in your tents and said, "The Lord hates us; so he brought us out of Egypt to deliver us into the hands of the Amorites to destroy us. 28 Where can we go? Our brothers have made our hearts melt in fear. They say, 'The people are stronger and taller than we are; the cities are large, with walls up to the sky. We even saw the Anakites there.'" ......42 But the Lord said to me, "Tell them, 'Do not go up and fight, because I will not be with you. You will be defeated by your enemies.'" 43 So I told you, but you would not listen. You rebelled against the Lord's command and in your arrogance you marched up into the hill country. 44 The Amorites who lived in those hills came out against you; they chased you like a swarm of bees and beat you down from Seir all the way to Hormah. 45 You came back and wept before the Lord, but he paid no attention to your weeping and turned a deaf ear to you. 46 And so you tayed in Kadesh many days—all the time you spent there.

(Deut 1:6-7;26-32;42-46)

DAY 304

"When you refuse his mind concerning you, he will change his mind on you. Just align your mind to his will".

29 Then I said to you, "Do not be terrified; do not be afraid of them. 30 The Lord your God, who is going before you, will fight for you, as he did for you in Egypt, before your very eyes, 31 and in the wilderness. There you saw how the Lord your God carried you, as a father carries his son, all the way you went until you reached this place."

32 In spite of this, you did not trust in the Lord your God, 33 who went ahead of you on your journey, in fire by night and in a cloud by day, to search out places for you to camp and to show you the way you should go. 34 When the Lord heard what you said, he was angry and solemnly swore: 35 "No one from this evil generation shall see the good land I swore to give your ancestors, 36 except Caleb son of Jephunneh. He will see it, and I will give him and his descendants the land he set his feet on, because he followed the Lord wholeheartedly."

Deut 1:29-36

DAY 305

"Never contend for what heaven has not given you. There is no victory for you in it".

5 Do not provoke them to war, for I will not give you any of their land, not even enough to put your foot on. I have given Esau the hill country of Seir as his own.

9 Then the Lord said to me, "Do not harass the Moabites or provoke them to war, for I will not give you any part of their land. I have given Ar to the descendants of Lot as a possession."

Deut 2:5,9

DAY 306

"He is a covenant keeping God. Keep your own part of the transaction, and it will be well with you".

19 When you come to the Ammonites, do not harass them or provoke them to war, for I will not give you possession of any land belonging to the Ammonites. I have given it as a possession to the descendants of Lot."

Deut 2:19

DAY 307

"Oh Lord! Hardened or free anybody's heart, that needs to be hardened or freed for my sake" (Prayer).

30 But Sihon king of Heshbon refused to let us pass through. For the Lord your God had made his spirit stubborn and his heart obstinate in order to give him into your hands, as he has now done.

Deut 2:30

DAY 308

"If you insist on having what God hasn't given you, the consequence is not always good".

5 Do not provoke them to war, for I will not give you any of their land, not even enough to put your foot on. I have given Esau the hill country of Seir as his own.

9 Then the Lord said to me, "Do not harass the Moabites or provoke them to war, for I will not give you any part of their land. I have given Ar to the descendants of Lot as a possession."

Deut 2:5,9

DAY 309

"Whatever God is instructing you to let go, and you refused, you could lose it all".

28 Sell us food to eat and water to drink for their price in silver. Only let us pass through on foot— 29 as the descendants of Esau, who live in Seir, and the Moabites, who live in Ar, did for us—until we cross the Jordan into the land the Lord our God is giving us." 30 But Sihon king of Heshbon refused to let us pass through. For the Lord your God had made his spirit stubborn and his heart obstinate in order to give him into your hands, as he has now done. 31 The Lord said to me, "See, I have begun to deliver Sihon and his country over to you. Now begin to conquer and possess his land." 32 When Sihon and all his army came out to meet us in battle at Jahaz, 33 the Lord our God delivered him over to us and we struck him down, together with his sons and his whole army. 34 At that time

*we took all his towns and completely destroyed[a] them—
men, women and children. We left no survivors.*

Deut 2:28-34

DAY 310

"If you don't own it, you will often do little or nothing to protect it (Abuse it). Have an owner mentality with what is God's (your life)".

12 The hired hand is not the shepherd and does not own the sheep. So when he sees the wolf coming, he abandons the sheep and runs away. Then the wolf attacks the flock and scatters it. 13 The man runs away because he is a hired hand and cares nothing for the sheep.

(John 10:12-13)

DAY 311

"He concerns himself not only with those in the house, but also those outside the house, because he is a father over all. Just come to him".

16 I have other sheep that are not of this sheep pen. I must bring them also. They too will listen to my voice, and there shall be one flock and one shepherd.

John 10:16

DAY 312

"You will carry others along with you easily, only when you look up to God".

13 I can do all things through Christ who strengthens me

Philippians 4:13

DAY 313

"When you look up, you can shoulder responsibilities beyond your ability".

13 I can do all things through Christ who strengthens me

Philippians 4:13

DAY 314

"Your response to the situations and circumstances around you, could determine and define your destiny. Just respond rightly and accordingly".

25 Let me go over and see the good land beyond the Jordan—that fine hill country and Lebanon."

26 But because of you the Lord was angry with me and would not listen to me. "That is enough," the Lord said. "Do not speak to me anymore about this matter. 27 Go up to the top of Pisgah and look west and north and south and east. Look at the land with your own eyes, since you are not going to cross this Jordan.

Deut 3:25-27

DAY 315

"What do you do, when shouldered with the responsibility of empowering someone to do that which you've been denied access to doing? Just do it graciously, there is still blessing in doing that".

27 Go up to the top of Pisgah and look west and north and south and east. Look at the land with your own eyes, since you are not going to cross this Jordan. 28 But commission Joshua, and encourage and strengthen him, for he will lead this people across and will cause them to inherit the land that you will see."

(Deut 3:27-28)

DAY 316

"Every expression of love, without commensurate giving, is just a mere lip-service".

16 For God so loved the world that he gave his one and only Son, that whoever believes in him shall not perish but have eternal life.

(John 3:16)

DAY 317

"When you lose sense of what is yours and what you have, you can hardly escape being jealous of what others barely have. You have a lot going for you".

25 "Meanwhile, the older son was in the field. When he came near the house, he heard music and dancing. 26 So he called one of the servants and asked him what was going on. 27 'Your brother has come,' he replied, 'and your father has killed the fattened calf because he has him back safe and sound.' 28 "The older brother became angry and refused to go in. So his father went out and pleaded with him. 29 But he answered his father, 'Look! All these years I've been slaving for you and never disobeyed your orders. Yet you never gave me even a young goat so I could celebrate with my friends. 30 But when this son of yours who has squandered your property with prostitutes comes home, you kill the fattened calf for him!' 31 "'My son,' the father said, 'you are always with me, and everything I have is yours. 32 But we had to celebrate and be glad, because this brother of yours was dead and is alive again; he was lost and is found.'"

Luke 15:25-32

DAY 318

"It's not always all about the much you have, but what you do with the little you have, that makes the difference. Maximize the little".

5 The apostles said to the Lord, "Increase our faith!" 6 He replied, "If you have faith as small as a mustard seed, you can say to this mulberry tree, 'Be uprooted and planted in the sea,' and it will obey you.

Luke 17:5-6

DAY 319

"Until the kingdom of God becomes your priority, you will never put things in perspective. Prioritize him over all".

33 But seek first his kingdom and his righteousness, and all these things will be given to you as well.

Matthew 6:33

DAY 320

"Be careful with your kind of request before the lord even when in despair, because he answers prayers.

28 Then Samson prayed to the Lord, "Sovereign Lord, remember me. Please, God, strengthen me just once more, and let me with one blow get revenge on the Philistines for my two eyes." 29 Then Samson reached toward the two central pillars on which the temple stood. Bracing himself against them, his right hand on the one and his left hand on the other, 30 Samson said, "Let me die with the Philistines!" Then he pushed with all his might, and down came the temple on the rulers and all the people in it. Thus he killed many more when he died than while he lived.

Judges 16:28-30

DAY 321

"When you refuse to eschew the obvious traps around you, hardly would you escape being trapped by them. Move away when you should and can".

16 One day Samson went to Gaza, where he saw a prostitute. He went in to spend the night with her. 2 The people of Gaza were told, "Samson is here!" So they surrounded the place and lay in wait for him all night at the city gate. They made no move during the night, saying, "At dawn we'll kill him."

3 But Samson lay there only until the middle of the night. Then he got up and took hold of the doors of the city gate, together with the two posts, and tore them loose, bar and all. He lifted them to his shoulders and carried them to the top of the hill that faces Hebron.

4 Sometime later, he fell in love with a woman in the Valley of Sorek whose name was Delilah. 5 The rulers of the Philistines went to her and said, "See if you can lure him into showing you the secret of his great strength and how we can overpower him so we may tie him up and subdue him. Each one of us will give you eleven hundred shekels[a] of silver." 6 So Delilah said to Samson, "Tell me the secret of your great strength and how you can be tied up and subdued."

21 Then the Philistines seized him, gouged out his eyes and took him down to Gaza. Binding him with bronze shackles, they set him to grinding grain in the prison. 22 But the hair on his head began to grow again after it had been shaved.

Judges 16:1-6, 21-22

DAY 322

"Your path can not be straight, until you submit your ways to the one who knows the way".

5 Trust in the Lord with all your heart and lean not on your own understanding; 6 in all your ways submit to him, and he will make your paths straight. [a]

Proverbs 3:5-6

DAY 323

"When you have so much of material possession, such that you think you don't need much of God, you will lose it anytime soon".

16 And he told them this parable: "The ground of a certain rich man yielded an abundant harvest. 17 He thought to himself, 'What shall I do? I have no place to store my crops.' 18 "Then he said, 'This is what I'll do. I will tear down my barns and build bigger ones, and there I will store my surplus grain. 19 And I'll say to myself, "You have plenty of grain laid up for many years. Take life easy; eat, drink and be merry."'

Luke 12:16-19.

DAY 324

"When you exclude God in everything you do, it's a potential open door for everything you do, to go wrong. Just get him involved".

18 "Then he said, 'This is what I'll do. I will tear down my barns and build bigger ones, and there I will store my surplus grain. 19 And I'll say to myself, "You have plenty of grain laid up for many years. Take life easy; eat, drink and be merry."'

20 "But God said to him, 'You fool! This very night your life will be demanded from you. Then who will get what you have prepared for yourself?' 21 "This is how it will be with whoever stores up things for themselves but is not rich toward God."

Luke 12:18-21

DAY 325

"Don't give up on your dreams, regardless of the surrounding hostility".

3 Now Israel loved Joseph more than any of his other sons, because he had been born to him in his old age; and he made an ornate[a] robe for him. 4 When his brothers saw that their father loved him more than any of them, they hated him and could not speak a kind word to him.

5 Joseph had a dream, and when he told it to his brothers, they hated him all the more. 6 He said to them, "Listen to this dream I had: 7 We were binding sheaves of grain out in the field when suddenly my sheaf rose and stood upright, while your sheaves gathered around mine and bowed down to it." 8 His brothers said to him, "Do you intend to reign over us? Will you actually rule us?" And they hated him all the more because of his dream and what he had said. 9 Then he had another dream, and he told it to his brothers. "Listen," he said, "I had another dream, and this time the sun and moon and eleven stars were bowing down to me."

10 When he told his father as well as his brothers, his father rebuked him and said, "What is this dream you had? Will your mother and I and your brothers actually come and bow down to the ground before you?" 11 His brothers were jealous of him, but his father kept the matter in mind.

Genesis 37:3-11

DAY 326

"He created you and all that is around you- just for you to take advantage of it, for his glory".

8 'The silver is mine and the gold is mine,' declares the Lord Almighty. 10 for every animal of the forest is mine, and the cattle on a thousand hills.

Haggai 2:8; Psalm 50:10

DAY 327

"Your future is history with God- It's all done, just step into it and have it".

10 I make known the end from the beginning, from ancient times, what is still to come. I say, 'My purpose will stand, and I will do all that I please.'

Isaiah 46:10

DAY 328

"If you can locate it somewhere in the word, and believe it in your heart- you will receive it somehow in your life".

19 God is not human, that he should lie, not a human being, that he should change his mind. Does he speak and then not act? Does he promise and not fulfil?

Numbers 23:19

DAY 329

"Don't just dwell on doing an incredible job of telling people where you are now. The story of your journey to where you are now, could be of some help too."

1 If the Lord had not been on our side—let Israel say—2 if the Lord had not been on our side when people attacked us, 3 they would have swallowed us alive when their anger flared against us; 4 the flood would have engulfed us, the torrent would have swept over us, 5 the raging waters would have swept us away. 6 Praise be to the Lord, who has not let us be torn by their teeth. 7 We have escaped like a bird from the fowler's snare; the snare has been broken, and we have escaped. 8 Our help is in the name of the Lord, the Maker of heaven and earth.

Psalm 124

DAY 330

"Never make pretense your reality, otherwise you will soon start believing your own lies".

9 Do not lie to each other, since you have taken off your old self with its practices 10 and have put on the new self, which is being renewed in knowledge in the image of its Creator. 11 Here there is no Gentile or Jew, circumcised or uncircumcised, barbarian, Scythian, slave or free, but Christ is all, and is in all.

Colossians 3:9-11

DAY 331

"If you can love people to the cross, God will do the conviction himself. Stop convicting and playing the judge in other peoples' life"

4 Love is patient, love is kind. It does not envy, it does not boast, it is not proud. 5 It does not dishonour others, it is not self-seeking, it is not easily angered, it keeps no record of wrongs.

1 Corinthians 13:4-5

DAY 332

"If it doesn't concern you, then you have no business reacting to it".

19 The teachers of the law and the chief priests looked for a way to arrest him immediately, because they knew he had spoken this parable against them. But they were afraid of the people.

Luke 20:19

DAY 333

"If what you do is being questioned, then it's a sign that it's getting somewhere and to some one. Just make sure, that it's the right thing you are doing".

20 One day as Jesus was teaching the people in the temple courts and proclaiming the good news, the chief priests and the teachers of the law, together with the elders, came up to him. 2 "Tell us by what authority you are doing these things," they said. "Who gave you this authority?"

Luke 20:1-2

DAY 334

"The gospel you live, will mobilize people for the gospel you preach. Just live it".

40 Peter sent them all out of the room; then he got down on his knees and prayed. Turning toward the dead woman, he said, "Tabitha, get up." She opened her eyes, and seeing Peter she sat up. 41 He took her by the hand and helped her to her feet. Then he called for the believers, especially the widows, and presented her to them alive. 42 This became known all over Joppa, and many people believed in the Lord. Act 9:40-42

13 When they saw the courage of Peter and John and realized that they were unschooled, ordinary men, they were astonished and they took note that these men had been with Jesus.

Acts 4:13

DAY 335

Until you begin to live what you preach, it wouldn't be long before many will begin to doubt what you say. Just live it.

15 "Watch out for false prophets. They come to you in sheep's clothing, but inwardly they are ferocious wolves. 16 By their fruit you will recognize them. Do people pick grapes from thorn bushes, or figs from thistles? 17 Likewise, every good tree bears good fruit, but a bad tree bears bad fruit. 18 A good tree cannot bear bad fruit, and a bad tree cannot bear good fruit. 19 Every tree that does not bear good fruit is cut down and thrown into the fire.

Matthew 7:15-19

DAY 336

"Only when you encounter the author of meaning, can you render meaningless what you consider meaningful to you in the world"

4 though I myself have reasons for such confidence. If someone else thinks they have reasons to put confidence in the flesh, I have more: 5 circumcised on the eighth day, of the people of Israel, of the tribe of Benjamin, a Hebrew of Hebrews; in regard to the law, a Pharisee; 6 as for zeal, persecuting the church; as for righteousness based on the law, faultless. 7 But whatever were gains to me I now consider loss for the sake of Christ. 8 What is more, I consider everything a loss because of the surpassing worth of knowing Christ Jesus my Lord, for whose sake I have lost all things. I consider them garbage that I may gain Christ

Philippians 3:4-8

DAY 337

"If the wisdom you claim to have about life does not humble you in life, then you are not wise enough".

13 Who is wise and understanding among you? Let them show it by their good life, by deeds done in the humility that comes from wisdom. 14 But if you harbour bitter envy and selfish ambition in your hearts, do not boast about it or deny the truth. 15 Such "wisdom" does not come down from heaven but is earthly, unspiritual, and demonic. 16 For where you have envy and selfish ambition, there you find disorder and every evil practice.

James 3:13-16

DAY 338

"Disorder and evil practices are the by-product of envy and selfish ambition. Check it and be careful".

16 For where you have envy and selfish ambition, there you find disorder and every evil practice.

James 3:16

DAY 339

"If you can overcome the fear, you will not see the need to lie. Just trust him".

15 And Simon Peter followed Jesus, and so did another[a] disciple. Now that disciple was known to the high priest, and went with Jesus into the courtyard of the high priest. 16 But Peter stood at the door outside. Then the other disciple, who was known to the high priest, went out and spoke to her who kept the door, and brought Peter in. 17 then the servant girl who kept the door said to Peter, "You are not also one of this Man's disciples, are you?"

He said, "I am not." 18 Now the servants and officers who had made a fire of coals stood there, for it was cold, and they warmed themselves. And Peter stood with them and warmed himself.

John 18:15-18

DAY 340

"Every think that makes you lie, is absent with God. Just trust him".

*1 In you, Lord, I have taken refuge; let me never be put to shame. 2 In your righteousness, rescue me and deliver me; turn your ear to me and save me.
3 Be my rock of refuge, to which I can always go; give the command to save me, for you are my rock and my fortress. 4 Deliver me, my God, from the hand of the wicked, from the grasp of those who are evil and cruel.
5 For you have been my hope, Sovereign Lord, my confidence since my youth 6 from birth I have relied on you; you brought me forth from my mother's womb.
I will ever praise you. 7 I have become a sign to many;*

Psalm 71:1-7

DAY 341

"It's not enough to be around people and not be lonely; without a genuine sense of connection, you will be".

15 And Simon Peter followed Jesus, and so did another[a] disciple. Now that disciple was known to the high priest, and went with Jesus into the courtyard of the high priest. 16 But Peter stood at the door outside. Then the other disciple, who was known to the high priest, went out and spoke to her who kept the door, and brought Peter in. 17 then the servant girl who kept the door said to Peter, "You are not also one of this Man's disciples, are you?" He said, "I am not." 18 Now the servants and officers who had made a fire of coals stood there, for it was cold, and they warmed themselves. And Peter stood with them and warmed himself.

John 18:15-18

DAY 342

"Excuses steal and waste grace. Stop giving one"

14 "Again, it will be like a man going on a journey, who called his servants and entrusted his wealth to them. 15 To one he gave five bags of gold, to another two bags, and to another one bag,[a] each according to his ability. Then he went on his journey. 24 "Then the man who had received one bag of gold came. 'Master,' he said, 'I knew that you are a hard man, harvesting where you have not sown and gathering where you have not scattered seed. 25 So I was afraid and went out and hid your gold in the ground. See, here is what belongs to you.'

26 "His master replied, 'you wicked, lazy servant! So you knew that I harvest where I have not sown and gather where I have not scattered seed? 27 Well then, you should have put my money on deposit with the bankers, so that when I returned I would have received it back with interest. 28 "'So take the bag of gold from him and give it to the one who has ten bags. 29 For whoever has will be given more, and they will have an abundance. Whoever does not have, even what they have will be taken from them. 30 And throw that worthless servant outside, into the darkness, where there will be weeping and gnashing of teeth.'

Mathew 25:14-15, 24-30

DAY 343

"You and where you are, are by-products of a lot of people's efforts. You need somebody in some ways".

9 Two are better than one, because they have a good return for their labour.

Ecclesiastes 4:9

DAY 344

"When the genuine concern of others become your genuine concern, God raises people who will show genuine concern towards you. Be genuinely concerned".

7 After the Lord had said these things to Job, he said to Eliphaz the Temanite, "I am angry with you and your two friends, because you have not spoken the truth about me, as my servant Job has. 8 So now take seven bulls and seven rams and go to my servant Job and sacrifice a burnt offering for yourselves. My servant Job will pray for you, and I will accept his prayer and not deal with you according to your folly. You have not spoken the truth about me, as my servant Job has." 9 So Eliphaz the Temanite, Bildad the Shuhite and Zophar the Naamathite did what the Lord told them; and the Lord accepted Job's prayer.

10 After Job had prayed for his friends, the Lord restored his fortunes and gave him twice as much as he had before.

Job 42:10

DAY 345

"Honour awaits you on the path of wisdom, but shame you cannot escape on the path of fools. Be wise".

35 The wise inherit honour, but fools get only shame.

Proverbs 3:35

DAY 346

"Uprightness with God is the key to upward moving in life".

7 He holds success in store for the upright, he is a shield to those whose walk is blameless,

Proverbs 2:7

DAY 347

"The weakest and the smallest are equally as important and significant as the strongest and the biggest. Despise nothing and no one".

15 Now if the foot should say, "Because I am not a hand, I do not belong to the body," it would not for that reason stop being part of the body. 16 And if the ear should say, "Because I am not an eye, I do not belong to the body," it would not for that reason stop being part of the body. 17 If the whole body were an eye, where would the sense of hearing be? If the whole body were an ear, where would the sense of smell be? 18 But in fact God has placed the parts in the body, every one of them, just as he wanted them to be. 19 If they were all one part, where would the body be? 20 As it is, there are many parts, but one body.

21 The eye cannot say to the hand, "I don't need you!" And the head cannot say to the feet, "I don't need you!" 22 On the contrary, those parts of the body that seem to be weaker are indispensable, 23 and the parts that we think are less honourable we treat with special honour. And the parts that are unpresentable are treated with special modesty, 24 while our presentable parts need no special treatment. But God has put the body together, giving greater honour to the parts that lacked it.
1Corinthians 12:15-24

DAY 348

"Your actions should promote friendship not division".

28 A perverse person stirs up conflict, and a gossip separates close friends.

Proverbs 16:28

DAY 349

"No opposition stands the test of time on your way, unless God is not involved in it".

21 On the appointed day Herod, wearing his royal robes, sat on his throne and delivered a public address to the people. 22 They shouted, "This is the voice of a god, not of a man." 23 Immediately, because Herod did not give praise to God, an angel of the Lord struck him down, and he was eaten by worms and died. 24 But the word of God continued to spread and flourish.

Acts 12:21-24

DAY 350

"God makes 'certain,' the 'uncertainty' of our hearts, when we trust him with it".

27 I prayed for this child, and the Lord has granted me what I asked of him. 28 So now I give him to the Lord. For his whole life he will be given over to the Lord." And he worshiped the Lord there.

1samuel 1:28

DAY 351

"Silence could be an ultimate weapon of power. Use your words wisely and carefully".

*27 The one who has knowledge uses words with restraint, and whoever has understanding is even-tempered.
28 Even fools are thought wise if they keep silent, and discerning if they hold their tongues.*

Proverbs 17:27-28

DAY 352

"Those after you will honor you, when you honor those before you".

30 "Therefore the Lord, the God of Israel, declares: 'I promised that members of your family would minister before me forever.' But now the Lord declares: 'Far be it from me! Those who honour me I will honour, but those who despise me will be disdained

1 Samuel 2:30

DAY 353

"Be expectant, for it will be when you least expected. Watch and be ready at all times"

45 But suppose the servant says to himself, 'My master is taking a long time in coming,' and he then begins to beat the other servants, both men and women, and to eat and drink and get drunk. 46 The master of that servant will come on a day when he does not expect him and at an hour he is not aware of. He will cut him to pieces and assign him a place with the unbelievers.

47 "The servant who knows the master's will and does not get ready or does not do what the master wants will be beaten with many blows. 48 But the one who does not know and does things deserving punishment will be beaten with few blows. From everyone who has been given much, much will be demanded; and from the one who has been entrusted with much, much more will be asked.

Luke 12:45-48

DAY 354

"The consciousness of your adversary's presence, should keep you on your toes".

8 Be alert and of sober mind. Your enemy the devil prowls around like a roaring lion looking for someone to devour.

1 Peter 5:8

DAY 355

"Hardly can you escape being dinner for the enemy, when you refuse the shield of God".

8 Be alert and of sober mind. Your enemy the devil prowls around like a roaring lion looking for someone to devour.

1Peter 5:8

DAY 356

"Ignorance can be a strong point of advantage for the enemy. Don't give him one, quit ignorance and be wise".

32 Then you will know the truth, and the truth will set you free."

John 8:32

DAY 357

"Ignorance is not a virtue, but a strong point of advantage for the enemy. Be wise".

9 Another reason I wrote you was to see if you would stand the test and be obedient in everything. 10 Anyone you forgive, I also forgive. And what I have forgiven—if there was anything to forgive—I have forgiven in the sight of Christ for your sake, 11 in order that Satan might not outwit us. For we are not unaware of his schemes.

2 Corinthians 2:11

DAY 358

"You are too saved to be a stumbling block in other people's lives. Resolve to add value and not subtract from others".

8 But food does not bring us near to God; we are no worse if we do not eat, and no better if we do. 9 Be careful, however, that the exercise of your rights does not become a stumbling block to the weak. 10 For if someone with a weak conscience sees you, with all your knowledge, eating in an idol's temple, won't that person be emboldened to eat what is sacrificed to idols? 11 So this weak brother or sister, for whom Christ died, is destroyed by your knowledge. 12 When you sin against them in this way and wound their weak conscience, you sin against Christ.

1 Corinthians 8:8-10

DAY 359

"When you insist on the details before obeying his instructions, you wouldn't go far with God.

He has and knows the details, and it's all working out for your good. Just obey".

8 By faith Abraham, when called to go to a place he would later receive as his inheritance, obeyed and went, even though he did not know where he was going.

Hebrews 11:8

DAY 360

"It's tragic to live your life without a deep sense of commitment to your purpose; frustration you can't escape".

If only for this life we have hope in Christ, we are of all people most to be pitied.

1 Corinthians 15:19.

DAY 361

"You don't have to run in the park or stay with the herds, so long as you know where you are going and where you belong and whose you are".

19 Though I am free and belong to no one, I have made myself a slave to everyone, to win as many as possible. 20 To the Jews I became like a Jew, to win the Jews. To those under the law I became like one under the law (though I myself am not under the law), so as to win those under the law. 21 To those not having the law I became like one not having the law (though I am not free from God's law but am under Christ's law), so as to win those not having the law. 22 To the weak I became weak, to win the weak. I have become all things to all people so that by all possible means I might save some. 23 I do all this for the sake of the gospel that I may share in its blessings.

1 Corinthians 9:19-23

DAY 362

"It's not enough to know what he did on the cross or what happened in the grave; connecting with it is the most important"

10 I want to know Christ—yes, to know the power of his resurrection and participation in his sufferings, becoming like him in his death, 11 and so, somehow, attaining to the resurrection from the dead

Philippians 3:10-11

DAY 363

"He promotes you to the level of your tolerance of pain and hardship".

27"Now My soul has become troubled; and what shall I say, 'Father, save me from this hour '? But for this purpose I came to this hour. 28"Father, glorify your name." Then a voice came out of heaven: "I have both glorified it, and will glorify it again." 29so the crowd of people who stood by and heard it were saying that it had thundered; others were saying, "An angel has spoken to Him."...

John 12: 27-29

DAY 364

"Until you put away some people, you will always have to put up with them".

33 Do not be misled: "Bad Company corrupts good character."

1 Corinthians 15:33

DAY 365

"It's not about what he can do for you but it's all about, what you can believe him for, because he can do all things"

28 When he had gone indoors, the blind men came to him, and he asked them, "Do you believe that I am able to do this?" "Yes, Lord," they replied. 29 Then he touched their eyes and said, "According to your faith let it be done to you";

Mathew 9:28-29

ABOUT THE AUTHOR

Lemun Yatu is a passionate lover of Youth ministry. He lives in Birmingham Uk, and serves in His church (Kingdom Life Apostolic Chapel) as a Youth Empowerment Minister. He is currently a doctoral researcher with University of Worcester business school UK- working on enterprise creation and entrepreneurial mind-set development. Sharing and leading his generation with the wisdom of God, into a growing relationship with Jesus, is the life that he enjoys and spends much time continuously developing. Wisdom keys for everyday is a collection of some of the inspirations that he receives every day, as he studies the word of God.

The book- 'Wisdom Keys for Everyday' will bless you immeasurably. Don't miss your copy.

Made in the USA
Charleston, SC
29 October 2016